BOREALIS
BOOKS

the dog says how

kevin kling

the dog says how

Borealis Books is an imprint of the Minnesota Historical Society Press.
www.borealisbooks.org

Photograph on page 181 by Mary Ludington.

The Minnesota Historical Society Press is a member of the Association of American
University Presses.

Manufactured in the United States of America

10   9   8   7   6   5   4   3   2   1

♾ The paper used in this publication meets the minimum requirements of the
American National Standard for Information Sciences—Permanence for Printed
Library Materials, ANSI Z39.48-1984.

International Standard Book Numbers
ISBN 13: 978-0-87351-599-3 (cloth)
ISBN 10: 0-87351-599-4 (cloth)

Library of Congress Cataloging-in-Publication Data

Kling, Kevin
    The dog says how / Kevin Kling.
        p. cm.
    ISBN-13: 978-0-87351-599-3 (alk. paper)
    ISBN-10: 0-87351-599-4 (alk. paper)
    1. Kling, Kevin, 1957– 2. Dramatists, American—21st century—Biography.
    3. Essays. I. Title.

    PS3561.L497Z46 2007
    812'.54—dc22
    [B]

                                                            2007023557

for Mary

the dog says how

the dog says how

on a motorbike

It all started because I wanted to fly.
I remember watching the barn swallows on my
  grandparents' farm
fork-tailed acrobats of the sky
darting in and out of rafters
following roads only they could see
living life just ahead of their bodies.
God I wanted to feel that,
a foot in two worlds.
So I got a motorcycle.

I love riding in the early morning before the earth
  stirs to life.

4 the dog says how

"I'm going to the store to get ice."
"Take the car,"
 she would've said had I woke her up
 and I'm off riding in the cool morning
 catching insects like a swallow,
 each gear takes me further from myself
 beyond obligations and administrations,
 linoleum, clocks, and committees
 so alive
 and then I see the car in the intersection.
 I hit the brakes
 and from my body I flew.

accident

When we were kids, my brother and I had a three-and-a-half-horse Briggs and Stratton engine. That engine went into everything: the minibike, then into the go-cart, then to a boat, to the go-cart, back to the minibike again. We'd bolt the engine to a frame and if there was time, we'd hook up the brakes. We lived by the theory, "Why stop if you can't get going in the first place?" This tactic usually ended up with one of us in the emergency room, where we were on a first-name basis with most of the staff.

Now, if my brother were getting stitched up I would sit in the back waiting room and read *Highlights* magazine. In it there were cartoons like the Timbertoes and the Bear Family—a family of bears so perfect they made the Family

Circus look dysfunctional. There was a page where one could search for the hidden objects, such as an anvil, a top hat, and a hatchet, all in a field of dancing unicorns. But best of all there was *Goofus and Gallant,* stories based on the lives of two boys, Goofus and Gallant. Gallant exemplified good behavior, Goofus bad. Bad behavior and good; Goofus and Gallant. The stories were written in the present tense; for example, Gallant cleans his room. Goofus sees if oily rags will burn in a window well. Gallant eats his vegetables. Goofus wonders what's inside a squirrel. What I liked was there was no recourse to either behavior. They were simply different approaches to life—and I was naturally drawn to Goofus. But I realized even then we are all made up of a little Goofus and a little Gallant.

On August 11, 2001, my Goofus got on his motorcycle and my Gallant put on his helmet. When I came to the intersection of Lyndale Avenue and Lake Street in south Minneapolis a car pulled in front of me and before I or Goofus or Gallant could touch the fully functional brakes, I crashed.

Over the next several hours I was in sections of the newspaper I'd never known and headed for one section I very much wanted to avoid. As I lay unconscious I had that end-of-life experience so often talked about. I never saw "the light," but as doctors were working to save my life, I was heading for this amazing sense of peace. At some point I was given the choice to continue on or return to this plane of existence where it was made clear there *would* be consequences. I decided to come back. At first it bothered me that I had returned. Why didn't I follow that peace?

Then I remembered Australia. In 1987 I was visiting Australia. It was so peaceful, so beautiful. I wanted to stay there the rest of my life. The problem was my visa was only good for three months. As the clock was winding down this woman named Rea said she would marry me so I could stay and aquire citizenship. I had just met her that day and she said, "Yeah, I don't care. I'll marry you." We were all set to go when at the last minute I said, "No. I can't go through with this. I have to get home. I need to be back where I can do something about this world we live in." I *need* tension. I mean, I'm the kind of guy who wears socks with sandals just because I know it ticks people off.

AT THIS POINT, there were people praying for me and sending well wishes. It's hard to deny the power of prayer when you're on the receiving end of it. I know it helped me heal. At times it was like waterskiing behind a powerboat. All I had to do was hang on.

I was also on morphine. Oh Morphine, you wonderful evil. Morphine is great because there is no pain. From running marathons, I know that when someone says you're looking good—you're probably not. But when I was on morphine people would say to me, "You're looking good," and I was thinking, "I already know it. And if I could get up or open my eyes, I'd bust a move right here." But oh, the price you pay. When morphine takes over, it takes over everything. It falsely takes charge, like Alexander Haig when Ronald Reagan was shot. It says, "I'M in charge now."

And then all reality is Morphine Reality. I had no idea what was real. You cannot convince me that half of my stay in the hospital was not on top of an Italian mountaintop or that there weren't two guys in the room spying on me dressed up like televisions.

At this time I was told my face would need considerable reconstructive surgery. In confidence a male nurse told me he thought I sustained minor brain trauma because my "head used my face as an airbag." My girlfriend, Mary, brought in photographs so the plastic surgeons could put my face back the way it was. There was some concern from my buddies, though, because in one picture I was holding the dog.

Friends started showing up. They brought books on tape to help me through. I found Harry Potter got me to sleep at night, and when I couldn't go to the bathroom, Tom Brokaw's greatest generation got the nation moving again.

Through all this time, my family was at the front: my mom, my sister Laura, and my brother Steve, who got me off a liquid diet by saying, "Wouldn't a cocktail weenie taste good right now? You know, in that red sauce?" At the time, my mouth was wired shut. I could tell by the slight smirk on his face that he was saying it to rile me but he was right. I *had* to have a cocktail weenie. I was out of those wires in a week; the doctors couldn't believe it. But when you have to have a cocktail weenie, you get one. Whoever said "me against my brother, my brother and me against the world," got it right.

After the accident, most of my life revolved around rehab and Velcro. There was extensive nerve damage done to my right arm, so I didn't have feeling or motor skills. And I have a congenital birth defect with my left arm; it's about three-quarters the size of my right arm, has no thumb or wrist, and is fitted with a plastic brace for protection. So up until now it's never done much work. I've taken to calling my left arm Scarlett, as in Scarlett O'Hara. Because before the accident, it was like, "Bring me a Coke with some chipped ice." But now it's got to do everything, poor Scarlett.

When I get depressed, I just take a look at our two wiener dogs. You'll never see more of a can-do attitude—in a more can't-do body—than a wiener dog. I know it doesn't matter whether you're Goofus or Gallant, you never know when something will happen. It's been said that God loved stories so much he created people so there would be an endless supply. I'm thankful I've been given the chance to rework my ending.

md carnival

When I was a kid, I played baseball in the summers. I batted first in the lineup . . . standing at the plate, teeth gritting, bubble gum in my cheek, and evil in my eye. Mr. Haynes, our coach, is yelling, "Good eye, Kev, good eye." Now, "Good eye, Kev," was actually code for "DON'T swing the bat, Kev." I was tiny—not little—tiny, and no pitcher could throw me a strike. I had no strike zone. I mean, the number on my shirt was tucked into my pants, so if I stood my ground, I walked to first every time.

"Good eye, Kev, good eye."

I wanted to hit that ball because in the stands was my friend Cheryl.

Cheryl was my best friend. She was teased a lot for

running like a girl—that way of running like Marilyn Monroe: arms out to the side, hips swaying, knees together, feet shooting out in all directions. Cheryl's body was changing. So people, mostly young boys, focused on that and missed out on how cool and funny she was.

"Good eye, Kev. Attaboy, Kev," yells Mr. Haynes.

Cheryl knew what I knew. Because of my left arm people made immediate assumptions about me. They called my arm withered or crippled, or asked, "What happened?" or said, "You poor thing." By the words they chose, I could tell whether they blamed God, my parents, the world, or themselves for my condition. And then with that information, I could get what I needed from them. It wasn't purposeful. It wasn't even conscious. It's just the way a kid works.

The pitcher tried to get one over. "Good eye Kev, attaboy."

I want to swing that bat. I decide the next pitch I am going to swing, no matter what. Even if I miss, it's only one strike.

One time Cheryl and I had a carnival for muscular dystrophy. We sent away for the packet that told us how to have a backyard carnival for your neighborhood to raise money for this worthy cause. I couldn't wait for the packet to tell us how to turn my ordinary backyard into the Greatest Show on Earth. I would be Jimmy Stewart, the jocular clown, and Cheryl, the beautiful rope-spinning butterfly. But when the packet came, the games didn't seem fun at all—some lame ring-toss game, a totally unfunny clown kit.

I mean, it was disappointing . . . like getting sea monkeys all over again.

Cheryl said, "This won't make a dime."

I asked what we should do. She said, "Give them what they want."

So, we made up our own MD carnival. We hung up blankets in the yard to create the big top and borrowed the mimeograph machine at school to make announcements of the upcoming spectacle. God, those announcements smelled good. On show day, I put on swim fins and a snorkel, stripped to the waist, took off my arm brace, laid on a table, and became . . . "Dolphin Boy." I had to be constantly sponged with a saline solution to keep my skin moist, like it was in my natural habitat—the ocean. To the wonder of the crowd, I performed math problems by means of honking a toy horn. I also pretended to have trouble breathing to add pathos to the situation and to show I'd rather be swimming free with my own kind. I was a *hit*. Then Cheryl did an exotic dance she called "The Dance of the Seven Veils," revealing "mysteries" of the Orient and bringing . . . "culture" to the unwashed masses. Oh man, it brought the house down. Word got out. Full houses every show. We could have run forever. We raked in the money for muscular dystrophy and had enough left over to pay the performers.

"Good eye, Kev."

Now the pitcher winds up and throws an obvious ball four. But this time I swing. I swing with all my might and the ball rolls harmlessly toward the shortstop. I run toward first base. The shortstop picks up the ball and heaves it to first. The ball takes a short hop off the first baseman's leg and into the outfield. I scamper to second and I don't even look. I am going to third; this may never happen again. Our whole team yells, "No!" I know Mr. Haynes is livid. The ball flies past me while I'm not even halfway to third, but it sails way over the third baseman's head. I round third for home. I hit home plate and who is running toward me? Not Mr. Haynes. (Oh no, we'll have a talk later.) No, it's my best friend Cheryl, running like a girl.

dogs

Dogs have been an integral part of our culture, from Cerberus, the three-headed dog who guarded the underworld, to Rin-Tin-Tin. To some extent, they are our creation. We have bred them to carry our burdens, guard our loved ones, hunt, herd, entertain. In ancient Egypt, the white on the chest of the Pharaoh hound was encouraged to reflect the light of the moon for night hunting. The long ears and wrinkles of bloodhounds are designed to hold scent for tracking. Some dogs were bred to keep queens warm on cold nights. Others worked as tireless sentries keeping predators at bay.

My uncle had hunting dogs and although he didn't hunt with them, he swore they were quality hound dogs. His backyard was full of dogs and old cars. Whenever he bought a new car he tore the doors off his old one, parked it out back, and it became the new doghouse. The dogs loved it and often sat in the front seat like they were going somewhere. My uncle loved to sit in a lawn chair framed in the proscenium of his garage door with a cold Schlitz tallboy beer and a cigarette, surrounded by his dogs. My dad said my uncle was the kind of guy who smelled "all the roses all the time." Sometimes he'd have a bar-b-que smoldering. His ribs were incredible. He told me the secret of good bar-b-que: "There's three things I never wash and one's my grill." One time while he was sitting around smelling the roses, he pointed at his dog and said, "Look at that darn dog. Been staring at that dead butterfly for two hours. Two hours. And I ought to know, I been watching it the whole time." My uncle couldn't have found a better dog. In his world it seemed time spent with his dog did not count against life. From my uncle I learned early the value of a good dog.

I love watching dogs dream. What are they chasing? In some cultures, on the night before the hunt, it was important to watch the dogs sleep. The one that dreamed he was already living the hunt was the dog to take the next day.

A friend of mine was pheasant hunting recently with her German Shorthaired Pointers. Three generations of hunting dogs. It was the puppy's first hunt and he was bounding all over the place. The oldest dog was thirteen and this was quite possibly her last hunt. She had been a tireless hunting companion throughout the years. The third dog was a four-year-old and in her prime. Although the dogs worked well, it was a slow morning. Finally a rooster got up and my friend shot and saw it drop up ahead. The three dogs took off, the four-year-old in the lead, followed by the veteran and then last came the puppy, excited but clueless. The four-year-old found the bird and was returning with it when suddenly she stopped and gently passed it to the older dog. The older dog took the bird several steps then stopped and gave it to the puppy to finish the retrieve.

SOMETIMES IT'S HARD to find the "beast" left in a dog. Princess, a Brittany Spaniel, lived with the mayor of a small town in North Dakota. I was asked to their home for supper one evening. I noticed when we sat down to dine there was an extra plate set; it turned out Princess had her own place at the table. What amazed me most about that dog was she waited until after grace before digging in.

Are we paired with the dog we deserve?

If that's true I immediately think of Charger. Charger was one of those big, goofy dogs that carries a log around all day— the kind of dog that would've joined the army for the food— a mutt with claims to all seven dog groups. Every year I'd watch the Westminster Dog Show and at the end when they'd announce "Best in Show," I'd yell, "Charger, you won, you won!" Charger wasn't very smart or if he was he hid it masterfully. One time when our neighbor started up his lawn mower Charger started barking and ran to the door. He thought I was pulling into the driveway on my motorcycle, even though I was sitting right next to him on the couch. When I said, "Charger, I'm right here," he looked at me like "how'd you do that?"

Charger never saved my life, or if he did, he never let on that he had, but when he passed away I cried buckets. The words of Kipling: "Brothers and sisters, I bid you beware, of giving your heart to a dog to tear." Despite this warning we do give our hearts to these creatures. Is this because dogs are our last connection to nature? For me the answer is simple: Charger was my friend.

NOT LONG AFTER Charger passed away my girlfriend, Mary, found a puppy. I told her I wasn't ready. Nevertheless, there stood Fafnir, a dachshund—a wiener dog.

I look at the floor next to him and say, "Who did that?"

"Oh," she says, "it looks like a little accident."

I walk around the house and there are more accidents than in a liquor store parking lot. I look at Fafnir—and I know you're not supposed to anthropomorphize dogs— but that face was definitely Lutheran guilt.

Mary says, "He's special. He's a show dog. He has papers and everything."

A show dog . . . No! My mind flashed to those dogs that resemble cleaning implements. All those perfumed, powdered, and pampered dogs—dogs the color of marshmallows in a box of Lucky Charms. I remember seeing a bumper sticker once that read, "Please don't tell my mother you saw me at a dog show. She thinks I play piano in a whorehouse."

Mary says, "Why don't you get to know him."

So Fafnir and I go out for a walk and I learn when people see a dachshund they have to yell, "A wiener dog!" like—a rainbow! A shriner! A shooting star! A clown! A nudist colony! Busloads of children cry out, "Look, a wiener dog!" as we pass my local motorcycle coffee shop. Now I'm waiting for the taunts and jeers from my biker friends, references to Fafnir as foodstuff for their larger dogs, when a leather-clad man named Zach steps up and says, "Nice dog."

I say, "What?"

"Yeah," he says, "That's a good-looking dog."

"Really?"

"Yeah," he says, "Good confirmation. And there's nothing that will go through a sack full of rats faster than a daschshund."

Wow. Now the guys are looking with new reverence, and I decide it's best to get Fafnir out of there before one of them says, "Hey, I happen to have a sack full of rats at home."

When I get home, I ask Mary when that next dog show is. And before you know it, I got more leashes than belts. I got a houseful of wiener dog doormats, gravy boats, knick-knack, bric-a-brac. Call me what you will, but when I put on a pair of pants, there's liver in one pocket and plastic bags in the other.

I remember a little prayer that goes, "Please Lord, make me the man my dog thinks I am." Ain't it the truth, when the world turned on Nixon he turned to Checkers. There's a passage in the American Kennel Club Show manual and the words refer to dachshunds, but I think they are words to live by. It says something like, "Scars achieved in battle will not count against contestants." Now that's got to make you feel better about yourself.

I've read that the Aztecs bred Chihuahuas to lead them across the great river into the afterlife. It makes sense. Where else would you entrust your soul than to something that would fight for you with that ferocity?

This story also gives me solace. I like to think that someday I'll see Charger again, waiting for me on this side of the river to cross together into peace. My guess is he's probably sitting in the smoking lounge right now with a bunch of Chihuahuas.

beaver in a box

The other day I was working with my neighbor Ben. He's about ten years old and we were breaking the glass out of an old storm door. I held the door frame over the garbage can and then Ben took a hammer and broke the glass into the can. All of a sudden Ben looks up and says, "Are there jobs like this?" And I said, "Yes, there are jobs like this."

I remember in my early twenties when I used to work at the chow mein noodle factory. It was a job through a temp agency where I was guaranteed twenty dollars a day whatever the work. I stuffed chow mein noodles into bags and after the first day I was offered permanent employment. I liked the chow mein noodle factory and they liked me, too, and called me "college boy" because I could read.

Every evening after work I'd race the band of daylight that stretched between the chow mein noodle factory and the Uptown Bar.

This was back in the late seventies before south Minneapolis was fixed up and gentrified. The bowling alley next to the noodle factory still hired human pinsetters, teenagers who smoked cigarettes, drank pop, and talked dreams, all the while straddling crashing bowling pins. Quick as a wink they disappeared anytime a carnival rolled into town. Next door to the bowling alley was the Ace Hardware store with the Zen-like sign in the window: "Help Wanted. Inquire Within." Past the hardware store sat a small brick building with a neon sign that hummed "Barbie's Sauna," where a man could get just about anything—except for Barbie or a sauna.

The Uptown Bar was a working-class bar. I push open the heavy steel door and enter the dark room. It took some time for my eyes to adjust but when they did I saw the familiar faces of people at their usual spots. B-girls sat up on the barstools—women who for a drink and a couple bucks would tell you how interesting you are. They were true sirens of their day and few could resist their art of conversation. Behind the bar were tickets to a meat raffle, a cash register decorated with bad checks, and a jar of pickled eggs old enough to vote. The clientele at the Uptown was mostly on the wide end of the economic pyramid, troubled men and women who sat over their highballs staring into the glass like ice fishermen waiting for a bite. The Uptown Bar was a hub of contemplation more designed for the *incuba-tion* of ideas than the actual hatching. There were guys who worked nights like Larry, at the slaughterhouse, and Scotty, who worked as a mortician's assistant, and Whispering Jesus, called Whispering Jesus because every time he stepped out on his bad leg he whispered, "Jesus."

One afternoon I was doing what we called "sitting around practicing for when we get old." I was with my buddy Larry. Ever since I've known him he's been missing some teeth and the bow from his Ray-Bans. I only know him from the bar. He's always there: summer, winter, fall. I saw Larry outside the bar once one summer day and it was horrible. It was like the sun was trying to kill him. I wanted to throw a coat over him and breathe smoke on him until I could get him back into the bar.

Larry and I watch the news together. The weatherman announced it was two below zero. First cold snap of the year. I worry for some of these guys. God knows where they go at night when this place closes. I guess there's a flophouse upstairs but nobody confirms it for fear of it getting shut down. There is an interview on the news with a guy— must be eighty if he's a day. He says he's from International Falls, the nation's icebox. He says, "Fifty years ago I moved up here for arthritis and this year I finally got it."

We all saw it at once. Out in the middle of traffic looking lost and scared was a beaver. We watched it cross the busy street one way and back the other. Cars screeched. Every once in a while he'd rear up to get a better look at his situation but he was clearly confused. His defenses for life in the wild were all but useless in this urban setting. Somehow this little guy had wandered into town. I wondered what body of water he could've come from. The Mississippi is over two miles away and the nearest lake a good mile, mile and a half. This beaver was clearly out of his element.

Now, after you've had a few beers one of two things happens. You either develop a great disdain for God's creatures or you become exceedingly magnanimous. Which is what happened to us.

"Gentlemen, we goda save that liddle fella," announced Larry.

"Poor guy," we all say.

So leaving our jackets inside and armed with only good intentions, we approach the beaver, speaking in falsettos, assuring him everything would be fine.

When you think of a beaver you might think of an industrious creature—kind of cuddly, an intelligent, happy worker. Couldn't be further from the truth. This thing had claws like razors and huge yellow teeth that were designed to fell a birch sapling in one bite. He emitted a hiss that made your knees weak. Worse yet, he obviously held some deep hatred for us . . . like he already knew us.

The beaver took the offensive. He gave a lunge that belied his winter fat. We feinted back. The beaver then picked his targets based on proximity. It was horrifying—like a mad ninja.

"The tail, watch the tail!"

"It's a deadly weapon!"

"I seen it on Mutual of Omaha."

The beaver continued on the offensive, taking advantage of the fact that he hadn't been drinking. And in no time he had us slipping and scattering for the safety of the bar.

From our perches back at the bar we watched the beaver finally settle into a defensive stance.

"I think he's sleeping. I bet we wore him out."

"Oh, he ain't sleeping. He's in a meditative state, more alert than ever."

Larry took a drink from his beer. "We used to have it, too, but it's evolved out of us somehow."

"How we gonna help him?"

"Sometimes nature doesn't want our help."

"But nature can't sense the danger, man. Look at the dinosaur."

"The dodo bird."

"The Baltimore Colts."

"Sometimes nature must run its course." It was Larry and this meant he was done helping the beaver. In his mind, the beaver had made his choice.

"Well, I for one am not giving up," said Scotty. "I got a buddy with a van. I'm getting it."

While he was gone Whispering Jesus went into the back room of the bar and came out holding a liquor box with a lid on it. He ran outside just as a rusted white van pulled up. The side door of the van slid open and with surprising speed they worked the beaver into the box, shut the lid, threw it in the van, slid the door shut, hopped up front, and were off over the hill. As we watched the one working taillight disappear, Larry turns to me and says, "How long you think it's going to take a beaver to get out of a cardboard box?"

larry

One Saturday I walked into the Uptown Bar. When I entered the bar something was off, I could tell even before my eyes adjusted. Then it slowly took form; Larry was nowhere in sight. I asked the bartender and he said that Larry was never in the bar on Saturday afternoons anymore. I asked where Larry went and the bartender didn't know, but he did know Larry would be back about four or five. I waited. Sure enough, Larry comes into the bar around five o'clock. I asked him where he'd been.

He said, "I was sitting with the cows."

"Larry, why are you sitting with the cows?"

He said, "To ask their forgiveness."

"Why do you need forgiveness from cows?"

Then he told me. . . .

"Whatever stories you've heard about a meat-process-ing plant, they're true. The conditions are deplorable. Four floors dedicated to the transformation of animal to meat. What arrives on hoof leaves in plastic. What's impossible to describe, however, is the odor. The rich, thick odor. Not a bad smell, but so thick at first it makes you sick—not from the smell but from the thickness. But after a time you get to craving that smell. You can't wait to get to the plant and breathe that air; it feeds you and all other air becomes insufficient."

Larry said, "I worked at the plant for five years. But you have to be very, very careful. A person can get used to al-most anything. A while back I quit and started visiting the cows on Saturdays and asking their forgiveness."

I asked, "What do the cows do?"

He said, "Mostly lay around, but you'd be surprised how forgiving they can be. . . ."

We ordered some beers.

"We need nature to sustain and forgive." Larry smiled.

And then the news came on.

taxidermy

When I was in the fifth grade we moved to the country. I didn't like it in the country. It was quiet and I didn't trust the quiet. Mom said not to worry, it was only my imagination, but that seemed to make it worse. My imagination? Good Lord, then it could be anything. My brother loved the country. He had a bow and arrow and played a game in the front yard with the neighbor kids where he'd shoot an arrow up into the sky. Then while the arrow turned around in the air and sped back toward earth, we'd test who could stay in the yard the longest. One time, he shot an arrow over our heads, and we were all standing there, looking into each other's eyes and pretending "there's not an arrow over my head."

"Well, there's not one over mine."

Finally, my spirit cracked and I ran for my life into the adjacent woods. The arrow came down right beside me and stuck in a woodpile.

"I got it," I yelled out.

And when I went over and pulled out the arrow, there was a chipmunk stuck on the end.

I said, "Steven, look."

He said, "Hey, I wasn't even trying."

As a kid, my brother, Steven, had the look of an angel; he carried the look of innocence. People refused to believe an evil genius walked among them. Except for that Halloween when he went as the devil, wearing one of those plastic masks and flammable suits they sold at the five-and-dime. After we got our candy he simply smiled and said, "See you in Hell." Like "see ya later." It was very disconcerting, like he had been given information.

Another time we were hunting with guns in the woods. Somehow we were given guns. Mine was on safety like it was in the five years I'd been hunting. And my brother, whose gun was definitely *not* on safety, was looking for an animal, something, anything to shoot at. All of a sudden this wood duck came flying through at fifty, sixty miles an hour, screaming through the woods. My brother caught it out of the corner of his eye, whirled, and fired from the hip, missing it by a mile. But the noise scared the duck. It swerved, hit a tree, and died! So we'd bring these animals home.

"Look, Ma! Look what we got today!" We were like cats.

Finally after a few years of this my mom said, "Oh, you boys. All right. I can't stop things from dying around you. It's going to happen. It's a given. But I can give you an appreciation for these animals." So she enrolled us in a . . . taxidermy class.

Taxidermy. Taught by Mr. Damyanovitch. Mr. Damyanovitch didn't teach taxidermy through the technical know-how. No, Mr. Damyanovitch taught through a method called: love. He would tell us about the duck. He would take the duck and lay it on the table and pet it, and tell us how it lived, what it liked to eat, and where it came from. Then he would part the feathers, and he'd make a slight incision and open up the duck. Then he would say, "See boys, it's just like taking a little man out of his suit." Then he would take the Twenty Mule Team Borax and pour it inside.

"Liberally with the Borax, boys. Liberally with the Borax."

Then he would put in a body and sew it shut, and preen the feathers back over the incision. Next he would put wires in the feet, then paint the feet and the bill, put in the eyes, set it on a log and say, "Now go to it, boys."

So we'd dive into our practice chipmunks with all the love our little junior-high fingers could muster. But when we got done, our little chippers didn't look quite as good as his duck had. But, after a while our chipmunks started to iron out okay. And over time they got better and better. And my brother seemed to have found a calling; he got really good. Steven started doing things with animals that the animals themselves would do in the wild if given the proper training. Incredible poses!

Now at the same time, we were in a Boy Scout troop. "Troop 584, good scouts are we." And we would have this yearly competition called "The Brookdale Show." The Brookdale Shopping Center would sponsor this show made up of Boy Scout displays. All the troops around the city would put on a different display and each of us would try to win the blue ribbon, and every year our troop won the blue ribbon with "winter camping." We set up a pup tent and piled drifts of fake plastic snow and stacked some logs with a spinning lightbulb behind them, like a fire, except for the orange extension cord running to the nearest outlet. And every year this lame presentation won the blue ribbon. The Brookdale Show was two weeks away. My brother and I had been waiting for this day. I got up in front of the troop and said, "Well . . . men, we can do winter camping like we do every year—and probably win another blue ribbon. Or, if you'd rather, we could do . . . taxidermy."

"Taxidermy? Taxidermy? Taxidermy, taxidermy, taxidermy, taxidermy, taxidermy!"

The kids were on their feet, shouting, "Taxidermy. Taxidermy." A father leapt up and said, "I think we should do winter . . . "—too late, my brother stepped in front of him and said, "Now go out and get those projects!" Zoom, the place was empty.

The next day in the woods you could hear guns calling

out in the distance, "Pop, pop . . . pop." Kids trying to get their "projects," projects at any cost.

They'd shout in the car, "Swerve, Dad, a project!"

Finally, the next week, in the middle of the troop meeting room, was this big table full of animals, projects—one for each child. And Steven and I taught them how to stuff with love. And they went to it. But we forgot that when we started into taxidermy, we couldn't turn out works of art either, and, of course their early projects were turning out kind of awful. We thought, "We don't have time to train these kids. We've got to think of something."

So, if a chipmunk didn't turn out quite right on one side, we'd have him lean against a log, so you couldn't see the problematic side. Or, we would paint a rural scene and set the animal in it, hiding what had gone wrong. Or, if an animal turned out really off, we would have the log as the main part and a tail coming out from behind the log like "he's behind there, somewhere."

Meanwhile, my brother was kicking out incredible, beautiful projects. One day he brought in a squirrel who had met its end kind of bad on the right side. And then he brought in another squirrel who had met its end kind of bad on the left side. My brother took those two squirrels, put them together, and made what we called "the quilted squirrel." Perfect. One stitch up the front, one down the back. It didn't matter that one was male and one was female. They fit! We put that one in front. We were going to win for sure.

And then a kid named John Stoner came in. John Stoner had a plastic Hefty garbage bag over his project.

"What's under the garbage bag, John Stoner?"

"You'll see at the end of the meeting."

"What do you mean?"

He said, "It's an unveiling."

We didn't know what he was talking about, but we did know that it was going to be good. John Stoner had been coming in with these squirrels that had nothing visibly wrong with them—they looked like perfect squirrels. We found out later that he was catching them in a Have-a-Heart Trap—a live trap—putting them in his garage, shutting the garage door, starting his dad's car, and asphyxiating the squirrels. One day his mother came in, saw her son in a running car in a closed garage and said, "John Stoner, what are you doing?"

And he couldn't say he was asphyxiating squirrels, so he said, "Uh, nothing." They sent him off for psychiatric care. But, before they shipped John Stoner out, he came into a meeting with this bag over his project. At the end of the meeting, he walked up, grabbed one corner and then another and . . . it was beautiful! John Stoner had taken four of those perfect squirrels and stuffed them to perfection. They were sitting around a log playing . . . poker. He even had visors on their heads and the skin of their arms rolled up like sleeves . . . with garters. They had cigarettes that smoked and the eyes on the squirrel with four aces were rolled back like, "Whoa! What a hand!" Oh, John Stoner.

We put his piece up front and with the help of Mr. Damyanovitch made a slide show presentation, "How to Stuff with Love." We set the theme from *Dr. Zhivago* as background music. So, we had the slide show, the quilted squirrel, and John Stoner's poker-playing critters. We were going to win for sure. We set up at the Brookdale Show and said to all the people walking by, "Look at this! Look at this!" Those people looked shocked, quickened their pace and averted their eyes; others blocked the eyes of children; some simply shook their heads and a few shouted in anger, "Look at that! Look at that! You kids should be ashamed of yourselves."

So the next year we did winter camping . . . and won a blue ribbon.

lightning

I'll never forget the time my father and I got hit by lightning. We were working on an airplane, a plane called a Bonanza. My dad always had airplanes when I was growing up. In fact, when I was born, my father was putting wings on a Piper Cub, and when he heard I was being born, he rushed to the hospital and held me for the first time with airplane goop and dope dripping from his hands. But the time we got hit by lightning, we were working on a Bonanza.

I was fourteen years old, lying in this puddle of water under the fuselage and my dad had just asked for a screwdriver. So I reached over to get one. It was underneath the airplane in the same puddle of water. I handed him the screwdriver when this big cloud, one of these big thunderheads that we get in Minnesota, went right over our heads, and I thought, "Oh no, we're going to get soaking wet," when Bam! This bolt of lightning shot through the puddle and hit my body. I felt it shoot through my organs . . . my stomach hit my liver hit my spleen—and I thought, "I've been hit by lightning! I've been hit by lightning!" And then I thought, "The fact I know I've been hit means I'm still alive."

I shout, "Dad, Dad, we've been hit by lightning!"

And he said, "Goddangit, that does it, let's go home." Farm boy. "Can't stay out here all day, we'll just keep getting hit by lightning."

A FEW YEARS AGO, my father passed away. I was at his funeral at this large table with my uncles, my brother, and my grandpa. We were talking about my dad, remembering him as vividly as possible because we knew we weren't going to get any new memories. We were holding on to the old ones as tightly as we could. So I decided I would tell them the story about how Dad and I got hit by lightning. I started into it when my Uncle Don sitting next to me said, "Wait a second. Wait a second. I've been hit by lightning. I've been hit three times."

He said, "Once you get hit by lightning, your chances of getting hit again increase by over fifty percent." He told us being struck by lightning is more the symptom than the problem. Then my brother said, "Uh, oh." He'd been hit by lightning. He'd been hit last summer at a gas station while pumping gasoline. Then my Grandpa says, "I've been hit by lightning." He'd been coming in from the fields with his tool belt on when, Bam! Lightning hit right beside him and he went up in the air and formed a fountain with himself and his tools. Then my Uncle Byron suddenly chimed in and said, "Wait a second, I've been hit by lightning." Uncle Byron said he'd been hit four times. Uncle Byron, who has a metal plate in his head from the war. He drives one of these metal Airstream trailers.

We said, "Byron, you're beggin' for it, pal."

So I found out right then and there that my uncles, my grandpa, my brother, my dad, and myself had all been hit by lightning. Or the day, as they put it, that I found out I was not adopted.

daddyland

This spring I'm driving through the countryside in northern Iowa. The green is so vibrant, the new growth seems to hold every color in the spectrum. It's almost too much for my rods and cones to bear. As evening approaches the rolling fields hold a softness like a Hopper painting. It's so peaceful.

I'm visiting a local deejay at a radio station out in the country. He's originally from the city and he says sometimes he'll be delivering the news, playing rock and roll, and he'll completely forget where he is. Then he goes to leave after his shift and he can't because there's a cow blocking the door.

I'm a first-generation off the farm. My dad grew up on a farm. We used to travel through his birthplace. He called it Daddyland. In Daddyland there was the ravine where he chased a badger with a two-by-four, the upside-down horse weather vane on top of the dilapidated barn, the one he had flipped over as a Halloween prank when he was ten—and to hear him describe Daddyland it was the most magic place on earth. You can have Pirates of the Caribbean. Take me to Daddyland.

I remember my grandpa, who farmed and could fix anything and always smelled like tractor grease, even in church. I loved that smell. He had a high laugh and always referred to our guinea pig as livestock. Could back up a car trailer into a thimble. At the State Fair we'd spend hours on Machinery Hill. We'd leave, he and my dad's shirts and pants covered in grass stains from crawling under, over, and around all the implements.

Grampa taught me to always carry a pocket knife and a pair of pliers. He taught me to be good to your neighbors because there will be a day you will need them. Farm kids taught me to smoke in the hay loft and how to ride on the backs of calfs as they bucked.

My grandparents had this old Bantam rooster that would chase my brother and me and peck us. We'd cry and Grandmother would yell at us to stay clear of her prize rooster. Only thing Grandma loved more was my sister. One day that rooster made the bad decision to make a pecking motion at my sister. Didn't even get her but we ate chicken that night. Toughest chicken I ever ate.

I learned from that rooster to be careful who you peck.

I'm driving through Iowa knowing this, too, is somebody else's Daddyland. New life is beautiful. Hope for the future. To the outside world this is home of the World's Largest Cheeto and the place where Buddy Holly's airplane went down. But there's plenty more to brag about. Kids here for the most part are happy. Lots of churches. With livelihoods relying on fickle weather, crop selection, and market values, you can see why faith plays a large role in farmers' lives. At one time our country identified itself through agriculture, pride in working the land. Robert Bly once said our country suffers from a neurosis that developed when we stopped working with animals.

Two hundred years ago this was the land of the Dakota, Ojibwe, Winnebago, Meskwaki, and Sauk. As settlers pushed west, trading posts set up a credit system with the Native Americans and when the bill came due often times it was collected through land acquisitions. Or the land was simply taken.

Now the same thing is happening to the family farms. Large debt is common. It actually costs more to produce the crops than market prices will bring. Only farms with massive equipment and acreage can turn a profit. Corporate farms. About two-thirds of the farmhouses are empty. There is a concern that most of the owners live on the coasts and this disconnect to the land may lead to unhealthy farming practices. There's a healthy mistrust of the outside world for good reason.

Now I drive along the high plain that runs through

southern Minnesota. I've been told it's the fourth-windiest spot in the world. It seems true. It is always windy and huge wind turbines dot the countryside. Hubert Humphrey, the senator and great filibuster, is from these parts.

My friend Dave's a third-generation farmer. At the State Fair I see his name on the plaque commemorating farmers from families a hundred years or older. I remember the year of all the flooding. We stood next to his field and Dave turned to me and said, "Bet you never saw whitecaps on a cornfield before." Nope. He quit trying to save his farm through farming, took a job in town, and now runs his farm in his spare time. He's taken to calling farming his art. He says it's the only way he could continue living there.

A few years ago, due to the declining population, the town processing plant threatened to close. Suddenly almost overnight there were people from Haiti, east Africa, Mexico, Thailand. The plant was saved and now the eclectic downtown restaurant scene rivals that of a city ten times its size.

Dave said he was listening to the radio the other day and he heard first-generation Americans talking about the struggles they face straddling two cultures. Suddenly his ninety-two-year-old grandmother came on the radio. He'd forgotten she was first-generation American. She was telling stories and laughing with the other guests in a way he said he'd never known. One girl was telling about going on a date and their car went into a ditch and when she arrived home late her father was hysterical. Yelling at this poor farm kid in Spanish. Dave's grandmother burst into laughter. Same thing happened to her only it was a horse and buggy and her dad was cursing in Swedish.

Last year Dave planted a field of sunflowers. His neighbors thought he was crazy. No money in sunflowers. When they asked him why he would do something so foolhardy he replied, "Because I can't afford a van Gogh."

We are on this land such a short time. The seasons turn. And will turn long after we're gone. There's a Native American saying: "We inherit the earth from our children." For my part I try to remember to carry a pocket knife and a pair of pliers, be good to my neighbors, and watch out who I peck.

dad's day

I'm hearing a lot of sound bites these days. It reminds me of being a kid when my dad would dispense his wisdom. We called them Dad's Sayings.

My dad passed away back in 1985. Enough time has passed to where places we would frequent that used to make me miss him now somehow bring him back to me. Brands of cars that he once owned drive by and I remember words of advice he dispensed from the front seat, like "Kev, the day you own a pair of wingtips is the day I stop worrying about you." Or "Kev, don't get killed just 'cause you know how."

I am now the age he was as I remember him best. Consequently many of the baffling things he did then are no longer mysteries, like constantly losing reading glasses or in a heated moment calling children or dogs by the wrong names. I keep looking in the mirror expecting to see him looking back at me. But I don't. I don't look like him.

But sometimes I do hear his odd phrases spring from my lips. Dad had a string of sayings that I use to this day, sayings that don't really make sense to me: Hotter then a three-dollar pistol. Colder than old Billy Ned. One time he told me I was about as funny as a hole in the fence. When he got off my brother's ten-speed bike one time he complained it was like a cheap hotel.

Cheap hotel? Three-dollar pistol? Who is Billy Ned?

Some of the phrases came from his farming background, like "You're so educated you're stupid." Grampa hit me with that one, too. Or when we couldn't get our go-cart to work Dad chimed in with "The loose nut is usually the one on the seat." When we said it worked fine yesterday he said, "That's what the farmer said about his dead mule."

Dads were more Old Testament back then, more brimstone than parable. Advice was often accompanied by a thwack on the head. My friend Russ Swansen's dad would thwack us on the head and say, "That's for what I didn't see." I used to think, "how does he know?" If a neighbor planted a cottonwood tree more than one dad was heard to comment that he should be shot. I grew up believing planting a cottonwood was a capital offense. The dad of our neighbors, the Sloans, used to mix and match his sayings, like "It ain't rocket surgery for crying outside." Or his famous

"I don't know whether to brush my butt or wipe my teeth."

One time my dad's skill in coming up with a saying was put to the test. We were going to swimming lessons. My sister and her friend were in the front seat with Dad, and my brother and I were in back. Dad was talking about something that was tight, a jar lid. He said it was tighter than . . . then he stopped. Both my brother and I were curious as to his saying. We'd heard many of his tighter-than analogies. One used an ingenious combination of a mosquito's anatomy and a rain barrel but none of these were appropriate for the present company. Finally he stammered, "It was tighter than the bark on a tree." My brother and I wept with laughter but had to give the old man credit for the cobbled saying.

When I do use one of Dad's obscure sayings sometimes I wonder if I'm getting it right. I have a friend these days named Misha. He was telling me not long ago that he told his nine-year-old son a joke: "A three-legged dog walks into a bar and says, 'I've come for the man who shot my paw.'" His son laughs and laughs. The next day Misha overhears his son talking to one of his little pals. His son says, "A three-legged dog walks into a bar and says, 'I'm looking for the man who shot my dad.'" Both the boys laugh and laugh.

The other day I was hanging out with my brother. We were taking his dock out of the lake and trying to get a rusted bolt off a section of it. My brother says, "This bolt is tighter than, . . ." then he paused a long time and said, "the bark on a tree." We laughed our heads off. My nephews are standing there soaking it all in. Perfect. Dad's phrase will live another generation.

So I'm thinking about Dad on this Father's Day. Now I know a three-dollar pistol is hot because it's stolen and a cheap hotel has no ballroom. I still don't know who Billy Ned is but I say it anyway 'cause as Mr. Sloan would say, if you can't stand the heat get off the pot.

view from the card table

There was never a time when I felt further from fear than Christmas Eve riding in the way back of a 1965 Impala station wagon. My mom and dad are in the front seat, my sister in the back, and me in the way back, surrounded by blankets and pillows and wrapping paper and packages and my brother, who is tolerable only when he sleeps.

We're on our way from Minnesota to Missouri to my grandparents' farm, where my grandmother waits "worried sick" until we arrive. We drive through the Iowa countryside past the white-topped farmhouses, the long hog barns, the barren fields, and chattering cornstalks. My mom is singing, "What did Io-way boys? What did Io-way?" We answer back, "She weighed a Washing-ton, Mom. She weighed a

Washing-ton." Mom had a song for every state in the union. I remember her song for Wisconsin: "I love to live in Wisconsin, and smell the dairy-air." Every time we pass a fence that's over six feet tall, my dad says, "Look at that, boys, a nudist colony." And we all run to that side of the car to try to get a glimpse at a nudist.

"Hey, Dad, what do nudists wear in the winter?"

"What do you think, boys? They bundle up. Nudists aren't stupid." Ah! those crafty nudists; of course, they bundle up.

We pull into a rest stop with two outhouses and a plaque declaring it an historic site. That's all it says: "Historic Plaque." The plaque never states why it's historic and I imagine a great battle in the cornfield with cavalry and Confederates and doughboys and Knights of the Roundtable, and the Iowa peasants—"With these two outhouses, we will never forget what happened here today!"

As night falls, we enter Centerville, Iowa, the blinking lights streaming down from the courthouse spire to the four corners of the courtyard, the candy cane cannon a spiral of blinking bulbs. And across the street is the pool hall with one of the pool tables pulled up to the front window and a Nativity scene set right in the center. My mom says, "That just doesn't seem right." We pull into the Texaco filling station for gas. Now, it's a little more expensive at Texaco, but with every fill-up, you receive a free Texaco Star Theatre Christmas Album: Bing Crosby, Johnny Mathis, Nat King Cole, Doris Day, star after star. And every year a different star tackles *The Drummer Boy*. This year, it's Patsy Cline. "Oh, that cute little Patsy Cline," my mom says. "How tragic. She makes me cry, makes me cry."

"No," my dad says, "you're thinking of Connie Francis."

"Oh, whoever. She makes me cry, makes me cry, makes me cry..."

And with the rear window framing moonlit Iowa like a black-and-white photograph, the rocking of the Chevy suspension and the AM radio gently telling me a storm is moving directly into our path, I pray to Jesus to remind God to ask Santa about that squirrel monkey in the back of *Spider-Man* for $9.99. Oh! and I want a *good* monkey, not like the neighbor's monkey, who had no sense of modesty according to my mom. No, I want a *good* monkey and a squirrel monkey, not a sea monkey. Those are a rip-off. Squirrel monkey. Now, earlier, I bribed my brother to ask my dad how much he loved me.

"Why, we love Kevin a lot."

"Nine ninety-nine . . . do you love him $9.99?"

"He is *not* getting that squirrel monkey!"

But in my prayer, I feel I got through to the reasonable Jesus, and soon visions of a squirrel monkey for $9.99 dance in my head.

When I wake up, I'm not in the station wagon anymore. It's Christmas morning and I'm upstairs in the farmhouse where my grandparents live and—puh puh. I'm spitting out—puh puh—little pieces of yarn from under a pink chenille bedspread. I wake up my brother and we run downstairs, the plastic feet in our pajamas slapping the oak floor. And there's Grandpa and he kisses me with that stubby farmboy beard, taking off a layer of facial epidermis. Then, Grandmother comes in. Grandmother scared me; she had those huge earlobes from wearing clip-on earrings her whole life . . . huge earlobes that scared me in a *National Geographic* kind of way. And Grandmother hugs me and she smells like every flower I've ever smelled at once. "Grandmother, let me go. There are presents to unwrap!" There are promises to keep. That's why we're here, for heaven's sake.

We run into the living room where the tree is piled high with presents. And my sister is the elf that year, because she can read, but she needs to sound out every word, and we can guess the name even before she's done, but she hangs in there 'til the last syllable, "Grrr . . . Grrraa . . . Grrrannma . . . Grrannma . . . Grandma . . . Grandma . . . Grandma . . ."

"Grandmother! It's Grandmother. Would you give her the present?"

And she hands Grandmother her present and she opens it up really slow, careful not to rip any of the paper, and she unveils this Russian fur hat from my dad, who claims he got it for my grandpa and must have got the boxes mixed up. Oh, but she won't give it up. No. She puts on the Russian hat and she looks good to me, like a Siberian empress with huge earlobes denoting royal blood.

Then, I dive into my presents, first opening all the boxes

that look like my brother's presents. Then, I hold up the contents and show him what he's about to receive. Next, come presents from Mom and Dad, because that's usually clothes or something I need, and then the last present is Santa's present—always the best—because Santa knows me. He knows the *me* of me. And I tear into the wrapping paper and reveal a box, which holds a plastic World War II P-40B fighter plane, a Flying Tiger, with a real gas-powered engine, hand controls, and a two-string guidance system. I mean, this is not a toy. This is something a *man* would play with. My brother and sister are, likewise, in heaven. My sister got a Chatty Kathy doll. When you pull the string, it talks, and the two of them are having a *meaningful* conversation in the corner. My brother's got his G.I. Joe and he's already twisting it, making screaming noises. And I look over at my dad, and my dad is smiling at me. My dad, the pilot in real life, is proud. He walks over and says, "Kev, what do ya' say after dinner, we fire that s.o.b. up?" That's when the fear sets in, because with my dad standing there, I'm going to have to fly this plane. I don't know how to fly this plane. Why, I know my dad could fly it. I even know my brother could fly it, but I know I can't. I know that I'll crash. I *know* I do *not* have the right stuff!

Now, I don't know how many people subscribe to the theory of predestination. I, for one, am a firm believer. I came across it during a reading of *Tristram Shandy,* where the protagonist, Tristram Shandy, describes his conception. Now, apparently, at the beginning of each month, his father,

Lord Shandy, performed two tasks. One was to wind the
family clock and the second was to perform his, well, hus-
bandly duties with his wife, Lady Shandy. It was during part
two of said ritual, and, in fact, at the moment of truth, that
Lord Shandy suddenly remembered he forgot to wind the
clock. It was due to this moment of indecision, this most
inopportune moment, this moment of his conception, that
Tristram Shandy attributes his own indecisiveness in life
and his need to sometimes fall off course. My own conception, I found out years later, happened when Pope Pius XII
was entertaining Liberace at the Vatican. Liberace called
it, "the single most inspirational moment of my life." Lord
only knows what the Pope was thinking, maybe singing to
himself, "I don't know how to love him," from *Jesus Christ
Superstar*—but I digress. Anyhow, if you subscribe to the
theory of predestination, which I do, and couple it with the
unfortunate astrological phenomena of Pisces with Aquar-
ius rising, it all leads to an overly sensitive, truth-seeking,
pencil neck that will *never* get that plane off the ground!

Christmas dinner. All the relatives start to arrive: Aunt
Charlene and Aunt Floy, two aunts that hug me, call me by
my brother's name, and say how much I've grown. Then,
they tell me how much I look like Uncle Bob, who is not
with us anymore. Aunt Floy starts to cry and Aunt Charlene assures her that Uncle Bob is better off where he is.
Hmmm. Oh! and then Uncle Johnny arrives, our favorite
uncle. Uncle Johnny, who whenever he points at something,
uses the middle finger, making the most obscene gesture.

"Which is the biggest barn, Uncle Johnny?"

"Well, I'd say it's that one there."

"Ahh!" We're cracking up. Then, we run to him with a map of Iowa. "Show us how to get home on the map, Uncle Johnny."

"Well, you go up here like this. I show you boys this every year."

My brother and I are laughing our heads off! Uncle Johnny is laughing, too, for reasons unknown. Oh! and I love the way my relatives from the South talk, that Midwestern drawl-l-l, that sitting-in-the-shade-tree-with-a-glass-of-lemonade drawl-l-l . . . the word "win-n-shiel-l-d wi-i-i-per" is its own sentence. I mean, there are words you have to sit down for.

They all file into the dining room around the big table, lengthened with extra leaves and covered with an embroidered tablecloth and candles and mistletoe napkins. And in the center, there's Santa with his reindeer. Oh, but it's not just Santa and reindeer; it's really a gravy boat. All the adults sit around the big table while all us cousins are out on the porch, where it's a little bit cold, and we're sitting around card tables. And there are our plates in front of us. Someone's already made my plate for me. Hey! I don't want some of this. I mean, the four basic meat groups are all represented. There's cranberry sauce, Jell-O, red (or it's not Jell-O), next to the mashed potatoes, where it can bleed into the side. My uncle stands up and announces grace. Uncle Dale is the preacher in real life, so everyone gets quiet. We bow our heads and hear a slight whistling sound, "Whrrr, whrrr, whrrr," and everyone knows that's Aunt Floy breathing through her nose. "Whrrr, whrrr, whrrr." Aunt Floy always had a clogged nostril and a little something in the other one, so it sounded like someone was running back and forth in the other room in corduroys. Uncle Dale blesses the food and our fellowship and that everyone made it safe. He prays in Jesus' name and calls him, "Our Savior." Our Savior. I start thinking, Jesus is our Savior? Don't you have to be in big trouble to be needed to be saved? I mean, doesn't a drowning person need to be saved? And Jesus is constantly having to come to earth to save us. What does that mean?

Then, I remembered the Meyers's cats. My friend, John Klein, was hired to watch the Meyers's two cats while they were out of town, these lazy, hedonistic cats. I mean, I never saw 'em move, but there were signs of destruction everywhere: chair legs shredded down to toothpicks, an acrid odor in one corner. But, you'd look at these cats and they'd sit there like, "Yes, I know. It was like that when I got here, too." Lazy, hedonistic cats. So anyway, Mr. Meyer told John to feed them twice a day and give them a treat "when you think about it." John and I laughed at what the treat might be. Then, one day, about a week later, we're riding our bikes, and I mention to John, "How's it going with the cats?"

John hits his brake and says, "The cats! The cats! Oh, the Meyers's cats! I forgot all about them."

I said, "They'll be okay, John. They can go a couple of days without food."

"No!" he says, "it hasn't been a couple of days. It's been a week! I forgot this whole week."

So we raced over to the Meyers's, and the cats were still alive, but, I mean, just barely. Luckily, the toilet seat was up, so they'd had something to drink. And when they saw John, they didn't think, "Oh, there's the guy who forgot us." No, they saw John as the one who saved them. Every time John came back from then on, those cats would see him and go crazy. "Oh, there he is! He's back." I wondered if that happened to God. "Earth. I forgot all about earth. Oh, my, me, I better get down there. Hey, what if they're mad at me? I know, I'll send the kid." And Jesus came down, and we all went crazy like the cats.

Uncle Dale nears the end of the prayer, and I know exactly what I'm going to do. As soon as he says, "Amen," I'm going for the gravy boat, because gravy is the one thing we have control over at the card table. Uncle Dale says, "Amen," and I go for the gravy, but my brother's already in it, ladling it up. That sinner had skipped the "Amen!"

Meanwhile, this little dog named Lady starts to bark, "Rooff, rooff, rooff, rooff, rooff, rooff, rooff, rooff." Lady is one of those little dogs with the rust stains in the eaves of her eyelids; she's always shaking like she's cold and barking like there's a fire. "Rooff, rooff, rooff, rooff, rooff, rooff." When Lady barked her high-pitched bark, she numbed something in the back of your hypothalamus. "Rooff, rooff,

rooff, rooff, rooff, rooff, rooff, rooff." My brother takes a piece of ham and starts to tease Lady. "Rooff, rooff, rooff, rooff, rooff, rooff, rooff, rooff," and right before Lady has a heart attack, he throws the piece of ham . . . and it sticks on the top of Lady's head! "Rooff, rooff, rooff, rooff, rooff, rooff." Now, she can smell the ham, but she can't see where it is. She's running around in circles! "Rooff, rooff, rooff, rooff, rooff, rooff, rooff, rooff," and then shoots through different parts of the house! All the cousins jump off the card table! Ahhh, Christmas at the Klings, and we start running around the perfect oval racetrack that's formed from the porch to the hallway, to the kitchen, to the dining room, and every time we hit the dining room, we're hit with a volley of threats, "In my day, you kids . . . hickory sticks . . . woodshed . . . G. Gordon Liddy." And as we hit the porch again, my brother can't resist grabbing a little bite of turkey but, in his haste, he knocks his plate off the card table and sends his Christmas dinner flying. By the time we arrive, Lady has secured most of the evidence, but my brother is in the corner hiccupping, crying the word, "Turkey, tur-key, tur-key," over and over. My mom fixes him another plate, sits him down, and says, "You see! You see what happens, you kids! Now, you *sit* back down and *enjoy* your Christmas dinner!" My brother stares at his plate unable to eat. I quietly remind him of the ham on Lady's head, and with tears on his face and turkey on his fork, he starts to laugh and takes a bite.

After dinner, I'm in the backyard with my dad and my

airplane sits in the driveway. Two control wires run to the middle of the yard. My dad walks up to the plane, hits the propeller, and wheeee, it whines like it's in pain. I want to faint but I know I have to stay at attention because I'm going to fly it after my father. My dad pulls one of the controls and the war bird rolls down the driveway. He pulls another control and it lifts up and flies over our heads. He pulls another control and it does a loop-de-loop. Another control and it banks into a turn. Then, he pulls another control and the plane goes straight up in the air and—Mayday! Mayday, Mayday! It crashes into the ground into a million pieces! I look over at my dad. He's looking at the controls. Obviously, that's where the fault lies.

Then, we both start cracking up. We both start laughing our heads off. I don't know why he's laughing but I know why I am, because I don't have to wreck my plane! My dad did it for me! We're standing there laughing. My brother comes out of the house and we're all three laughing. I mean, face it, none of our toys made it through Christmas Day. My brother's G.I. Joe was a vet inside of two hours. My sister's Chatty Kathy, the string in its back hanging out, just sat there staring at my sister, who was having a one-sided conversation, which was fine with her. My dad turns to me and says, "Well, Kev, I happen to know where Santa got that plane, so we can always get you another one."

I look up and say, "Or a squirrel monkey."

We're called into the house for leftovers. We fix turkey sandwiches and put them on paper plates and set them on trays in front of the TV, trays that are specially designed to eat while you watch TV. This is one of the first colored TVs—a Zenith—that hums as it warms up, which we know now is radiation. If we would have known then what we know now, we could have probably cooked the turkey right there on our laps. We watch *Ben Hur* with my mom and dad laughing as my brother and I count the polio vaccination scars on the galley slaves and gladiators. When it's over, we climb upstairs, put on our pajamas with the feet in the bottoms, and crawl into our beds with the chenille bedspreads and go to sleep.

In the morning, we wake up, take our broken toys, our pillows, and our blankets and load 'em into the way back of the station wagon. We climb in and drive across Iowa, along the trail mapped out by Uncle Johnny, back to Minnesota, back to home.

drive-in

When I was a kid there were milkmen who would deliver dairy products every morning in the neighborhood. If you didn't get out early and collect your delivery, a Basset Hound named Huckleberry usually came by and licked the butter and the top off your cream. Then he'd lie down in the road. Nobody ever hit him with a car; for one thing, there weren't as many cars back then and the ones that were there knew to drive around him. We'd pass Huckleberry on the way walking to school and on the way home for lunch.

After finishing our sandwich or SpaghettiOs we'd quick go to the TV set and turn on Casey Jones. This was a cartoon show hosted by the railroad legend Casey Jones and his sidekick Roundhouse Rodney. Casey mostly introduced the cartoons while Roundhouse was always doing pranks and riddles, trying to make Casey laugh. But the best segment of all was Kids Korner, where Roundhouse would demonstrate how to make stuff that kids enjoy . . . like a sword made out of two slats from a snow fence (that one didn't go over so well with the parents), or when he taught us how to make whistles out of willow sticks. The whole neighborhood was alive with whistles . . . for days, parents yelling at first with anger—"You kids stop that this instant!"—then two days later breaking down and pleading, "Please, for God's sake, stop."

The best thing about Roundhouse was his hat. He wore this beautiful round hat, like a little dunce cap. One day Roundhouse told us how to make a hat like his. All you had to do was take an old felt hat and put it over a football, bring it into the bathroom, and then turn the hot on in the shower. Close the door and leave it inside for half an hour. Take the hat and ball out of the steam, let it cool, and voilà, a Roundhouse hat. We quick grabbed our dad's Sunday felt hat and made it into a Roundhouse hat. That night my dad saw his good Sunday hat, now a Roundhouse hat, proudly displayed on my brother's head. Instead of being grateful, as we had imagined, he became very upset and enraged. This confused us not only because of the obvious improvement we'd brought to its style but also because he could still use it on Sunday, as we would only need it during the week for school. I think a lot of dads felt the same because the next day Roundhouse said, "Stop making hats. Please forget I ever showed you." I never saw a Roundhouse hat on any other kid after that.

Sometimes on weekends we'd put on our pajamas, pile up in the back seat of the car with blankets and pillows, and head to the Starlight Drive-In movie theater. Dad popped a grocery bag full of popcorn; we brought all kinds of soda pop. We'd park in the movie lot and put the speaker in the window. That window crack always let in some mosquitoes and every speaker sounded like there was a piece of wax paper inside, but, man, we were in heaven. A car full of teenagers pulls in front of us and so many kids climb out of the trunk it looks like a clown car. We get permission to go to the playground they have in front of the concession stand. It's a really lame playground—gravel under the swingsets, slivers in the teeter-totter—but it's full of kids in pajamas.

"Did you make a Roundhouse hat?"

"Yeah, me too, worst decision of my life."

"Me too."

We hit the swings. A cartoon is on but we can barely see it because it's not quite dark yet. When it looks like an animated box of popcorn announcing six minutes left to the feature, we hurry back to the car in time to see the first cartoon. It's one of those special features put out by Disney as a community service. This one features the Seven Dwarfs and an alarming statistic about the diseases carried by mosquitoes. The dwarfs, under the instructions of a humorous voiceover, drain the oil out of the crankcase of their car. I never knew they had a car. Then they take the bucket of oil down to the lake and dump it in. A microscope shows a mosquito larva smothering in the oil. Of course by the end Dopey is covered in oil and the proud dwarfs sing their way home. My mom turns to my brother and me and says, "Don't even think about it."

As it becomes dark my dad says, "Look kids," and we looked up to see birds—night hawks, swallows, and bats eating mosquitoes. "Get 'em boys. Let's take care of business," says Dad. He loved aerial combat movies. Then the fogger comes by, a small lawn tractor pulling a fogging machine for the bugs, and my sister and her friend are dancing behind it like fairy princesses, spinning and twirling like magic in the DDT.

Then the cartoon box of popcorn says its show time. I hope it's a Clint Eastwood. No music ever tortured the speaker like Ennio Morricone's. But I rarely saw the feature. The next thing I knew I was waking up in my own bed and Huckleberry had already made his rounds.

Nowadays the Starlight is covered in grass. The speakers have been clear-cut, leaving metal stumps lined up in front of the screen, which is missing panels and looks like a sad face. You can't go back, I know that, but the other day I heard whistles the neighbor boys made. They played them straight for two days until the neighbors cried, "For God's sake, stop." I have a Basset Hound now and he has to wear a leash so he won't sleep in the road. But sometimes I'll let him lick the butter. I know it's not as good as stealing, but he really likes it.

mom's purse

Long before there was *Jackass: The Movie* there was me and my brother.

WE WERE ALWAYS going to the emergency room for something "done in the name of science." One time we pulled into the hospital parking lot—it was my turn to get stitched up—and were headed for the door when we heard a honking horn. We turned to see a van with the side door wide open and a woman inside giving birth to a baby. Attending her was a doctor and a nurse but obviously this was as far as she was going. What drew our attention to the van was the honking horn. In the front seat were two young boys, one honking the horn furiously while the other dumped the contents of the glove compartment out the passenger side window. Between pushes the woman was yelling, "RILEY, KNOCK IT OFF."

I remember my mom staring blankly at the scene. I was thinking, "See Mom, you have normal sons."

THERE IS ONE MAY weekend in Minnesota that is the annual Clash of the Titans: Mother's Day versus the fishing season opener. Mom and fishing are two great loves going head to head. The choice is a dilemma that nourishes the essential demons of Lutheran guilt. Because look, you gotta Mom and you gotta fish. So, if you're like me, you're either loading up your gear or sitting in the boat, hoping you mailed the card in time and thinking your gonna make them fish pay for what they're doing to your mom. And over the weekend in those long lulls, when the bobber sits there like a painting, all those times Mom wiped away the tears, held you when you were scared, and nursed you back to health, come creeping in like holes in the boat.

Voices emerge from the lapping waters.

"What are you kids doing in there?"

"What's going on? It sure is quiet."

"You better not be doing what I think you're doing."

When mom did find out what we were doing her reprimands always held an amazing sense of optimism. Like, "What if everybody did that?" Yeah, what if everybody did roll their brother up in a carpet 'til he screamed and looked like a giant insane Pez dispenser? That would be great.

Another one of her favorites was "There is a time and a place for everything." Oh, so the issue isn't that we blew up my sister's Barbie doll with an M-80? It's more of a time and place problem. Amazing. Then there was mom's purse, a mystery wrapped in a conundrum wrapped in Naugahyde. The magic bag of Felix the Cat had nothing on mom's purse. At any given time it was a hospital, a smorgasbord, a washroom, or a beauty parlor. Whatever the situation called for, the purse held the answer. Got a cut? Dirty face? Try a little spit on a hanky.

The Sloans's mother carried old bubble gum wrappers. When something stinky would roll through, she'd hand out the gum wrappers to hold over your nose.

But I remember one year mom's purse was put to the test. Every Christmas we went from Minnesota to Missouri to visit our relatives. Our station wagon would be full of presents and we'd sing Christmas songs. It was the best. But this year my sister had decided to stay at college. Then my dad announced he wouldn't be able to get away either. My mom said she didn't care. She was spending Christmas with her family, and my brother and I were going with her. We loaded up her car and on Christmas Eve, headed through Iowa, where we were immediately pulled over by a cop for going ninety-five miles an hour. I think that cop had a mom, too, because after that look my mom shot him, he turned right around and walked back to his car. Case closed.

As we were approaching Des Moines, the first snowflakes began to fall. All of a sudden a clunking, tearing racket emerged from under the car. It sounded like a piano and a plumber falling down the stairs.

We wheeled into a truck stop where we learned the transmission had gone, and they weren't sure if they had the parts. Even if they did, we were going to be there a long time. We went to the cafeteria and my mom held her head in her hands. Being in junior high I did what I could to make matters worse.

"If Dad was here . . ."

"Well, he's not."

I knew I was supposed to act older, but I didn't. It was pretty clear by then our family was falling apart and I wanted to cry. So did my brother. Just before the tears started to flow, my mom reached into her purse and pulled out a drinking straw still wrapped in paper. She held it upright, tore the paper off one end, and slipped the paper down the straw until it made like a tiny concertina at the bottom. She removed the paper and laid it on its side. Then she put the tip of the straw into her water, pulled out a drop and said, "Look boys, the magic snake."

She dropped the water on the scrunched paper and it began to move like a snake. Then it stopped. I would have to say it was the lamest trick I ever saw. We sat there staring at the wet piece of paper when my mom put her hands over her eyes and started shaking. In our family it wasn't proper to comfort someone. You generally let them work through it. But mom was shaking pretty badly. As I reached toward her I noticed she was laughing her head off. The tragedy had hit bottom and was rapidly heading for the surface. Then my brother and I started laughing, too. I grabbed two white non-dairy creamer containers, shoved 'em in my eyes and sang, "The sun will come out tomorrow."

My brother showed how long he could keep a milk bubble on the end of his tongue, and we continued our talent contest until the table was strewn with garbage, and then the waitress asked my mom, "What if everyone did that?" Then we laughed and my brother's talent-milk shot out of his nose. Mom, like a candle to the dark.

So on fishing opener, whether we catch fish or not, the boat may have my body. But my heart is with my mom.

snow day

"Academy of The Holy Angels. Ada-Borup, public and parochial; Adrian, public and parochial."

I wake up to the sound of the radio in the kitchen. "Aitkin, public and parochial."

WCCO, good neighbor to the north, is announcing school closings. "Albert Lea, public and parochial." It's also been announced that Minnesota has just been hit by the snowstorm of the century. I'm only nine years old and this is already my third snowstorm of the century. I look over at my brother, still asleep on his twin bed, which is identical to my twin bed. When he sleeps, he looks so harmless, so innocent. I get a feeling of actual affection for him when he's out cold. I look over at my shirt and pants in the corner of the room. I quick get out of bed, run and grab them, thinking "time me, time me." I get back under the covers and hold them until they warm up. "Alden-Conger, public and parochial."

In the kitchen, mom is staring out the window at the new blanket of snow, leaning on one elbow on the counter, holding a cup of coffee.

"Forest Lake, public and parochial." She's waiting for the Os.

"Osseo, have they said Osseo?" I say.

"Not yet," she says.

"I hope . . ."

"Shhhhh . . ."

"Orono, private and parochial."

Please, oh please, Osseo. Say Osseo. I'm about ready to make a deal with God when—"Osseo, public and parochial."

"Yahoo, so long suckers, no school and it's a weekday, and I'm not sick." There is a God, there is, there is.

"No school today," says mom.

"Boy, don't I know it."

"Now you'll have time to spend with Grandmother."

"Ahhhh, nooooo."

Grandmother is visiting from Missouri and granted, I don't see her very often, like twice a year maybe. And I do love her, I swear, but this is a snow day. Come on, it may never happen again. I gotta be out in it. Something big is going to happen out there and I need to be out in it.

Then I notice Grandmother standing in the kitchen in her robe. Grandmother, public and parochial. I think she's heard everything. I'm busted. She comes over and hugs me.

"I have some things to do this morning," she says to my mom. "We can catch up at lunch."

I know by mom's look I'm supposed to argue, but I can't. I'm sorry, warden, but the governor called and I gotta go.

My brother and I get down to the hockey rink just as Paul Puncochar finishes shoveling off the last bit of the storm of the century. It's time for hockey. We choose teams, sing the national anthem, make the public address—"there's no smoking in the arena"—drop the puck, and it's nonstop action.

I have to use my mom's figure skates. At first the guys laughed because the skates were white and had a ring of grey fur around the top. But because of the grip-toes on the front, I could beat anyone in a short burst of speed. Besides, nobody had skates that actually fit, or were new. In fact, Hank and Frank Haines, the twins from down the block, had racing skates with the long blades. They were fast, but they couldn't turn. The blades were too long, so they had to go straight 'til they hit a snow bank and then turned around.

Nobody had equipment either, like shin pads. So we made the rule "NO RAISES." The puck had to stay on the ice. After about five minutes nobody followed the rule, and besides, if you broke it, the penalty was the other team saying, "Knock it off, NO RAISES." And action would continue.

As a kid the worst pain I can think of is a raised puck to the ankle. Especially in white figure skates with fur on top. And Pat Gilligan takes a slap shot from the point. The puck, like a deadly, ankle-seeking missile on a mission from hell, finds its bony target. Ahhh! First I'm nailed in the ankle. Ahhh! Then my toe catches and I fall forward and hit my head on the ice. I feel a coldness flowing up from the point of impact. It spreads through my head and as I turn and look up, the world is framed in blue. My body tingles and there's a single high note in my head, and I want to throw up. My brother stands over me and says the magic words to take away pain. They're from an episode of *Star Trek*: "A Vulcan would not cry out so." But the magic words don't work. I'm in pain. I'm going home.

I get there just in time for lunch. SpaghettiOs are usually my favorite. No other food was the same color, texture, or flavor as SpaghettiOs, made by a real chef. And nothing cuts authentic Italian food like grilled cheese with Velveeta and a large glass of milk. But when I look in my bowl of SpaghettiOs they seem even more vibrant than ever. Then they start to do a strange little dance in the bowl. I told mom I felt sick. She looks at my eyes and immediately calls the doctor.

I have a concussion. I have to stay awake for a whole day and night because, according to the doctor, if I go to sleep, I might never wake up. I decide to stay awake—for Pat Gilligan. Pat Gilligan, you're dead meat.

That night I want to sleep so bad. Mom takes the first

shift to keep me awake. She reads from the storybook Bible, Moses after Moses after Moses; then we watch Johnny Carson and she explains the need for Ed McMahon. Then I need sleep. Grandmother takes the second shift.

"Grandmother, help. I'm going to sleep." And every time I do, the Lord's Prayer goes through my head and when I hit the part, "if I should die before I wake," it scares me, but not enough to keep my eyes open.

Grandmother wraps me in an afghan and says, "Are you comfy?"

"Yes, but that could mean death, Grandmother."

But then she starts in. She tells me of growing up in Holland, learning to skate behind a chair along the canals. I say, "That's how I learned to skate." She knows. She tells how she ran away from home at age sixteen and went to the city. Grandmother tells me about being a flapper. In my delirium I imagine her arms going up and down really fast. Her hairdo was called a bob. I imagine it named after our neighbor Bob, who was bald and used to say he shampooed with Mop and Glow. She tells me about Grandpa, and Mom as a little girl, and by the time she got to me, the sun is coming up and I hadn't died.

The next night we're huddled around the TV watching *Gilligan's Island*, the one where the monkey is throwing plates made of explosives. There is a fire going in our fireplace. I looked over at Grandmother. She is looking in the fire with that look she has when she is talking about meeting Grandpa. Gilligan was on TV. I wonder who is in the fire.

We go to bed that night. I finally get to go to sleep. Sleep. School tomorrow. I don't even care. I throw my pants in the corner. My brother gets in his twin bed.

"Good night, Steve."

"Shut up."

No problem. In a couple of minutes he'll be out cold and I'll love him again.

marching band

I have to admit, musically, I pretty much plateaued in junior high. I always thought it was because a week after I got my trumpet, my brother threw a pencil down the bell, which—seemed to me—gave it a nice, smoky, jazz sound. But the band director saw it differently and had to have a heart-to-heart talk with me.

"Kevin," he said, "you know, there are many other avenues of artistic expression that you might want to explore."

"No."

"Kevin, you can't stay in the band."

"But sir, I can't join choir . . . I'm tone-deaf."

"Yes," he said, "I know."

"And art is so messy and Home Ec scares me. There's a song in my heart; it's trapped—and tone-deaf and has no rhythm—but it's there, I know."

And I cried and cried and he softened up and left me last chair in the worst band: We were called the "Cadet Band"— all seventh graders, and me, a ninth grader.

Now, Mark Twain once said that Wagner's music was better than it sounded. *Everybody's* music was better than it sounded when the Cadet Band played it. When listening to our band it always felt like there was a bee trapped in your head somewhere that couldn't get out. At the walls of Jericho, we could have been like the band that prevented structural damage—and stopped the walls from tumbling down—because I'm sure the Canaanites would have said, "Just stop. Stop it. We're coming out."

I have to claim that I was part of the problem. Whenever we came to the end of a song the band would finish, but I always had some more music left to play. Or I would finish my music and put down my horn and the band would keep going. Then I would have to quick pick up my horn and pretend I had more to do. One time I was playing "Hogan's Heroes March," an old basic, and lo and behold, I finished at the same time as the band. A miracle. Then the director said, "Very good, band, and now we'll play 'Hogan's Heroes.'" I thought we *were* playing "Hogan's Heroes." I still don't know what they were playing.

The best time of year to be in band was the summer.

I loved marching band. For one thing, everybody got to play. So I was mixed in there with Kim Feller, first chair state champ. The drummers, all hockey players, were tough and cocky and sinewy. And the music . . . this was not regular band music—no. In marching band we played bona fide pop hits. Everyone's song could be a marching band song—Simon and Garfunkle "Hello darkness, my old friend" (boom boom rat a tat boom rat a tat). Frankie Valli "Silence is golden, golden" (tat tat rat a tat boom tat tat). Starland Vocal Band "Afternoon Delight" (boom tuka tuka crash tat-e-tat). Jimi Hendrix "Purple Haze"(b-dah b-dee b-doh b-doo tat tat). Ted Nugent "dog eat dog. . . ." (bugeda-bugedabugeda crash). Even, "Tequila."

Best of all were the uniforms. School colors in black and orange, ancient and wool, for both seasons. High Beefeater fur hats that had to be cinched in so tight your eyebrows sat just above your upper lip. I remember bringing my uniform home. I was so excited, but I was kind of small, so they'd given me a girl's uniform . . . with *darts*. Darts sewn into the chest and even worse, when I put it on the darts went in, accentuating my concave chest and giving me a look like I was the mold for a 1957 Cadillac bumper. My mom, bless her, stayed up all night taking out the darts, and I was set for the summer.

The summer of my ninth grade, Mr. Sand, the high school director, announced we'd been invited to a parade, a real parade. The Old Milwaukee Days Parade in Wisconsin. Before this year our only parade had been the Osseo

Lions Club Parade . . . and that was only four blocks long
and we followed a float from the retirement home. I guess
it was a float. There was a pick-up truck with four people
sitting in the back around a card table playing bridge, and
they never looked up. I wondered if someone shouldn't tell
them, "Hey, you're in a parade, wave or something." But,
then again, maybe being in a parade hadn't been their idea
to begin with. But now we were headed for the Old Milwaukee Days Parade. Three miles long and we would be judged
against other bands.

Mr. Sand also announced he was going to turn us into
something. We thought we were already something. We
drilled for a month. "Come on you lazy good-for-nothings.
You call that an embouchure? Put that horn to your lips
and give me twenty."

We marched into the night up and down, under the street-
lights of Osseo. Kids were sitting on the corners, taunting us.
Corner after corner . . . "lines tight, eyes forward!" . . . and
Mr. Sand turned us into a well-oiled machine.

We made the drive to Milwaukee and spent the night
in a motel. In the morning the entire drum section was in
the motel office promising they'd "never do IT again," and
that they would "pay for IT." They seemed a little foggy and
their uniforms a bit off, like they were in the Italian Army.

We made our way to the parade site. There were busloads of bands from all over the country, eyeing each other
over. As we lined up, I almost started laughing. We had this
whipped. Mr. Sand's plan was flawless. A block away we

would start with "Hogan's Heroes," then as we approached the judging area, feint back with "MacArthur Park" as a palate cleanser. Then we'd hit 'em hard with the classic hit "25 or 6 to 4." It was brilliant.

I looked up front at our drum major, Mike Marachek, an imposing figure in size fifteen boots and an all-white uniform. He was haughty, powdered, pampered, rouged, and ready for action. In his white Beefeater hat, he looked like a giant, beautiful Q-Tip. Then we lined up and suddenly an official jumped in front of our drum major.

"Hold it, hold it," he said, one hand indicating "stop" and the other waving in. "Bring 'em in."

And we watched as they escorted the forty-horse Clydesdale team in front of our band—amazing, majestic, imposing beasts pulling a large wagon of beer barrels. And *no* clean-up crew. Which meant in ten minutes we were going to be marching down the middle of Milwaukee in ninety-eight-degree heat with the forty-horse fun factory mining every step of our way.

Mr. Sand handed out salt pills. "Take these only in case of an emergency." We all immediately took the salt pills.

THE PARADE STARTED. In no time my lips were parched. Those wool uniforms were heating up. My black Beefeater hat felt like a solar collector. Just before the judging table the front-row flute section hit something slick on the pavement. Watching those Beefeater hats drop was like out of a scene from *The Patriot*. It was horrible.

But just as fast they were up again, hats now at various angles and one player missing a flute but "miming" the instrument. Somehow we held it together through "Mac-Arthur Park."

"Now," shouted Mr. Sands, "we've trained for this."

He was right.

Woodwinds and horns snapped into place, the low brass moved in for cover, drummers—untucked and defiant—fired steady rounds of timpani, and out front, leading the charge, the giant Q-tip, size fifteen white boots, kicked up to the sky.

I decided not to look down no matter how or what I felt. Mr. Sands kept shouting words of encouragement, and although I couldn't hear him, out of my periphery I could see his jaw moving like a loose hinge, his face going from red to purple, a big vein popping from his forehead.

We passed the judging area, our heads high.

" . . . Twenty-five or six to fo-oo-our. . . ."

AFTER THE PARADE, we lay next to the buses in the parking lot. Uniforms from all over the country lay scattered around us—royal blue, gold, red, white, and now mixed in with it all, our orange and black.

"That was the worst," a veteran member proclaimed. Only the drummers looked the same as when we started.

Mr. Sands came around to everyone individually and told us he was proud.

"You won't need rockin' to sleep tonight, Kling," he said.

"No sir."

"Next year we might try you on tuba." Next year. There would be a next year.

I looked down at what was once a spotless spat. "Mr. Sand, look," I said.

"Throw 'em away son, just throw 'em away. You did good, boy, real good."

nutcracker

I remember the first piece of art I ever sold. I was in college. One night I saw Audrey, a flute player with the band, sitting at the local pub with a friend. I introduced myself and announced I also had an interest in the arts, that I had shown quite an aptitude in a drawing class. Audrey seemed preoccupied, but her friend wondered if I had some sketches in my room.

"Why yes, I do. I do have some sketches in my room." She then wondered if I'd show her my portfolio.

"Of course," I said, and we were off.

When we got to my room I took out my portfolio and to a somewhat surprised Audrey's friend, I displayed my sketches, especially the human figures, and said how the hands and feet give me the most trouble as you can see by the shoes and mittens. She was impressed. And then, when I felt the evening couldn't get any better, she said she wanted to, you know, buy a painting.

"Of course," I said.

Then she leaned into me and whispered, "It feels good to buy art."

I said, "I know."

I have never forgotten that evening, the evening I knew I was an artist.

The first performance art I ever bought was a viewing of Mary Gilligan's appendix scar during recess behind the brick pump house. It challenged me.

I FIRST LEARNED about being an artist during Ms. Keller's third-grade class. Through the luck of alphabetized seating I was able to watch Robin Johnson create a series of paintings of her house.

During show-and-tell, Robin Johnson showed the pictures she had painted of her house. They didn't look anything like the place where she lived, but she was a way better artist than the house she had to live in, so we let it go. I loved the pictures, the colors, the eye for detail, the confidence in the composition. I had to have one of her houses. So I paid my lunch money for one. Then I learned how good it felt to own art and to support someone I admired. That lunch money prompted Robin to create more houses she never lived in and in no time most of the third-grade lockers housed Johnsons.

. . .

SO EVEN AT THIS early age, I knew I was an artist. It seemed like there were those of us bursting with art . . . and that expanding art looked for the easiest way out of our bodies. Through its flow one determined what kind of artist you would be. A painter's hand was always moving, a singer's breath took on the rhythms of the world, and a dancer, a dancer's whole body got to move.

Every year our grade school held two assemblies. One was a visit from NASA. An aerospace engineer displayed the marvels of space travel, highlighting the event by dipping a grape into liquid nitrogen and then breaking it with a hammer. This swayed many toward the space program. The other assembly was a dance production of *The Snow Princess*. I'd seen people dance on TV, but never thought they were real. They were too perfect. Then the snow princess came to school. The beautiful snow princess, while breaking ties with her oppressive father, not only danced on stage, but up and down the aisles. And as she spun past, I noticed she had dark leg hairs poking out of her white tights. This wasn't perfect. This meant the snow princess was real—and a modern woman. The NASA guy came back every year. We never saw the snow princess again but she had already awakened in me a yearning that would not quiet.

Our school taught art and music, but dance was not encouraged. I played third-chair trumpet in concert band until the band director suggested I try another form of expression.

I informed him I was already interested in dance. He said, "Kevin, you may want to try pottery, coil pots."

"There's no future in coil pots. I want to dance," I said.

He rubbed his face with his hands as he liked to do before coming to his point.

"Kevin," he said, "you have no rhythm. When you clap to a song you're a bit behind, and your clapping looks like you're trying to catch something."

"I am," I said. "The beat. If I can catch it, maybe I can keep it."

He rubbed his face harder and let me stay in band, all the while trapped in the body of a dancer.

THIRTY-FIVE YEARS later I get a phone call. It's Lise Houlton, director of the Minnesota Dance Theater. They want me to perform a small part in the production of Loyce Houlton's *Nutcracker*. I am so excited, I say yes without thinking. For rehearsal she said I'll need a dance belt and ballet shoes.

The next day, full of the holiday spirit, I run to the dance store in town. I announce to the shopkeeper that I'm in the *Nutcracker*.

"Oh, which one?"

"How many are there?" I said.

She's in the one in St. Paul and her daughter is in another one for kids. It turns out everyone from the Joffrey Ballet to the Humane Society has a version.

"I'm in the one with the Minnesota Dance Theater," I announce, "and I need shoes and a dance belt."

She gets the shoes, but before she gets the dance belt she looks at me and says, "I think you're an eight."

This worries me. I know three of my sizes and *none* of them are an eight. She brings me a box and I take it home. In case you've never worn a dance belt, they're the evil little brother of the jockstrap. They're super-tight elastic, for holding everything in place. The first time I put one on, I made a face like my dad made the time he sat on my brother's ten-speed bike. If you don't think dancing makes you feel like a man, put on a dance belt. You know you're a man.

Now that I had my gear I decided to look at the story. The plot of the *Nutcracker* is like something that Hunter S. Thompson would have conceived when crossing the Nevada border.

The dance is based on the story "The Nutcracker and the Mouse King," written by E. T. A. Hoffmann. It's about a little girl in a loveless household fighting bloody battles against a Mouse King with seven heads. In the new version there is a Christmas party at the house of a little girl named Marie. Her godfather, Herr Drosselmeyer, presents his gift, a beautiful nutcracker. Her little brother, Fritz, soon grabs the nutcracker and breaks it. Okay, normal so far. Soon the guests depart, and the family goes to bed. But Marie sneaks back to the tree where strange things begin to happen. The tree grows; the room fills with mice, led by the mighty Mouse King. The nutcracker comes to life and engages the mice in battle. The nutcracker then turns into a prince and he and Marie are welcomed by dancing snow-flakes. As a finale, the Sugarplum Fairy and her Cavalier dance a pas de deux. Marie awakes from her dream and finds herself by the tree with her beloved nutcracker.

In rehearsal I learned I would play a character called Madame Bonbonniere and also the Judge hosting the party. I felt confident about playing the Madame. She has lots of makeup, a huge wig, stilts, and children dressed as mice who startle her as they emerge from her dress. It's fun and wacky.

But this Judge presents a problem. Joining me on stage will be members of the American Ballet Theatre and beautiful dancers from the Minnesota company. I'll have to actually dance. Besides, tights are not kind to me. My friend Buffy Sedlachek says my knees look like I'm smuggling walnuts. And after years of writing, my body is in the shape of a question mark, instead of the preferred exclamation point. My body doesn't say, "I'm here!" It says, "I'm here?"

Not to be daunted, I employ an old stage trick. When in doubt, get a mustache and have the size of the mustache grow in an inverse ratio to the talent of the performer. I looked at the mustaches in stock and then had the costumer go out and buy me a jumbo one. Then, I dug out my college makeup kit, and found a base called "Leading Man Pancake." It's the color of humans that I imagine are found in remote sections of Sicily. I have never known anyone to use it, but with this mustache—the cross between a helicopter and a dog—riding my upper lip, and "Leading Man," nobody would be looking at my legs.

Opening night was spectacular. The Judge went off without a hitch. I had some trouble with the Madame's wig and almost stepped on a mouse child, but even that seemed to flow unnoticed.

In the receiving line following the show, a patron was going down the row of dancers gushing praise. "How wonderful, how beautiful." When she got to me she said, "And you, what a good sport." Good sport? Hmmm. Later on at the party, a mouse child told me she liked last year's Madame Bonbonniere better than mine. Children can be so . . . honest. I was crushed. Later that night the little boy playing Fritz came up to me and gave me a hug. He is six years old and already an amazing dancer. I asked him his secret.

He said, "You know what you need to do?"

I said, "What?"

He said, "Every dancer has a diamond on their chest. You need to show that diamond all the way to the back of the theater."

After that night I let my art fly out the diamond on my chest. I was never very good, but you would've never guessed it by my joy. My favorite part about the show was watching the kids in all the wings offstage and the looks on their faces as the principal dancers took the stage. And by the looks on their faces, this was much better than smashing a grape with a hammer.

circus

When I was twenty-six, I ran away to the circus, toward the marvelous adventure that awaited anyone who answered the newspaper ad for auditions. What was promised was six months creating a circus and performing in towns down the Mississippi River, from Brainerd, Minnesota, to New Orleans. What it foretold was adventure—Huck Finn–style, lazy days, and hanging out with river folk, and the wild and romantic life of a circus performer.

I called the number. "I'd like to audition."

"Oh, alright."

"Are there animals?" I asked.

"No animals, we're not that kind of circus. It's a puppet circus," said the man.

"Okay. Do we live on the boat?"

"No boat, we have buses. We're looking at a boat."

"Oh."

"The pay is $25 per week."

"Oh. Okay."

"We will provide housing; tents mostly."

"Oh."

"And food. All you can eat."

Say no more. I'm there. This is better than I hoped.

At the audition I told them I could puppeteer, walk stilts, and play the baritone horn, and they were thrilled. I left confident enough to quit my job at the chow mein noodle factory, find a horn, and someone to teach me how to walk on stilts. And that's how I became part of the Heart of The Beast Puppet and Mask Theatre Company and the "Circle of Water Circus."

One morning in May we all met in a church to move supplies to a farm outside of Alma, Wisconsin. There we would build the circus. I looked about the room at my fellow performers. They looked like people from another time. "Hippies," we had called them. I thought the last one had died of the disco fever in 1978. But here they were, probably the largest gathering of their kind in the area. Except for one man, dressed in a suit on a hot day. He sat directly across from me, hunched over, smoking, his "Type A" leg shaking violently. Did he have to come? These hippies were one thing, but this man scared me.

I discovered he was married to the trombone player, who

seemed very kind. Maybe she knew how to calm him with kind words, a song, or a cookie if he got agitated. Still, I would keep a watchful eye on the man with the shaky leg.

We spent the morning loading gear, and then we had our first meal. I was starved. Then out came what I call the "terrible Ts": tofu, tahini, tabouli, and tamari. When we finished I was starved. What, a vegetarian circus? My God, we'll die.

We were told to start loading equipment and I noticed the man with the shaky leg loading a Weber bar-b-que grill. I imagined he was going to cook up bar-b-que along the river—pork shoulder and seasoned ribs, steaks and chops and brats. He turned to me and said, "Just in case we see any wild monkey." I didn't care, and I realized suddenly I would have to befriend the scary man.

And I did . . . on the farm. During the day, we built puppets and rehearsed the show. At night we took bike rides to the local tavern trying to stretch out our twenty-five dollars. It was after one night at the tavern that the shaky-legged man and I found ourselves walking along the dirt road back to the farm. My bike had a flat tire so we were pushing the bikes. He told me he and his wife, the trombone player, were expecting a baby. They were going to name her Alma if it was a girl, after the town in Wisconsin. Actually, her name would be Alma Marina, taken from the beautiful waters and high bluffs. He hoped they would have a girl, because if it was a boy, he would be called Nelson Cheese Factory, in honor of the local industry.

One day it was announced we had a boat. Well, sort of. It was a houseboat from Lake Minnetonka, and there was some question as to its sea worthiness. Navigating a lake is one thing, but river currents and eddies and barge traffic is another. One solution was to hire a captain to reduce our risk. We put it to a vote and narrowly agreed to hire the captain and buy the houseboat. Those of us who voted for the boat would be reminded of this time and again.

We celebrated that night by firing up the Weber. Thirty bratwursts hit the flames and thirty brats were gone. Somewhat of a miracle considering there were only four claimed meat eaters. I think in the Bacchanalian frenzy there was some backsliding, but who could blame them with the news of a boat.

Our captain arrived shortly. He was rough and tough, hard as nails, a Vietnam vet. Every other word was something like my grandpa said when a tractor fell on his toe. This swabby could get us through, no doubt. We got the houseboat. Before we left he said he hoped it would be no inconvenience but during the trip he would be making the change from a man to a woman. He'd never felt comfortable as a man and now he was making the change. I knew I started to love this group when no one batted an eye.

Fine with us, let's hit the river.

We performed in Brainerd, St. Cloud, the Twin Cities, La Crosse, Wisconsin, and Clinton, Iowa. Every couple weeks the Captain would head back to the Twin Cities for counseling or injections—or charm school. Charm school was the worst because for a week he wouldn't open a door for himself or steer the boat. They had turned him into a 1950s starlet and we had barges and eddies. One foggy night the Captain was creeping us down the river. We heard a low horn.

"Good Lord," he said. "That's a barge. Try and see it."

But the fog was too thick. We heard it again, the horn blaring through the soup.

"Go up top and see if you can see anything."

I scrambled up to the top to find a musician practicing the bass clarinet horn. I told the Captain it was a guy practicing his horn. He opened his mouth and a few hundred dollars worth of charm school went out the window.

When we hit St. Louis a great surprise awaited us. Jacques Cousteau was there filming a special on the Mississippi. We really wanted to meet him. There was his magnificent boat, the Calypso, its bowsprit graced with a beautiful mermaid leading the way. Our boat had deteriorated quite badly. Someone needed to constantly bail. The engine was acting up. We spruced it up as best we could, got some paint, and wrote "Calapso" on the side in huge letters. I got a woman's bowling trophy from a thrift store and we lashed her out front as our bowsprit. Jacques Cousteau was not amused. We tried to meet him several times but were informed he had wine tastings and research that took precedence.

I was upset, or "bummed out" as my fellow travelers would say. I wanted to meet the man, inventor of the aqualung and French voiceovers. Not long after that our poor Calapso sank where the Ohio River meets the Mighty Miss and our captain went back to Minneapolis for his operation to become a woman. We were now traveling in school buses. The close quarters, lack of protein . . . I started to lose it.

We all had meltdowns. Sooner or later, everyone lost it on the trip. This was mine. I decided this was it. I was quitting. I had about five dollars on me, so I went to the Greyhound station and started begging to let me ride. I was pleading to the ticket agents like they were the American Consulate.

"Please, just please, put me on a bus."

I figure once on one, I could stow away, get into a compartment, anything. But I'm not going back to lettuce sandwiches.

Then I saw the trombone player in the station. In her hand was a spare rib—meat with sauce. It looked incredible. Linked to her arm was Shaky Leg, and then a friend who was visiting them who said he was running for mayor of Milwaukee. He had treated them to a rib dinner, and when they heard I'd made my break, they'd come looking for me, with bait. They handed me the rib and I took a bite. Unbelievable. Ambrosia. Then I noticed she had another one. What I didn't notice was we were walking out toward the car, and by the time I'd finished my third rib, I was snuggled in my tent.

We did finally make it to New Orleans. The show was

well received and I met a group of lifelong friends, family really. And like family it was certainly a group I wouldn't have chosen as my people but one to which I now count my blessings I belong. I'll never look at the river the same either. Every time I cross it I have a feeling for its power and beauty. That river lived up to every metaphor written. At times sitting on the deck of the Calapso, surrounded by high bluffs, passing a barge or swimming kids or a fisherman, it was impossible to tell what decade, what century held our journey. The gift of that river, as Shaky Leg would say, lies deep in the "ever changing, never changing muddy waters." That said, one day I will get the trombone player and old Shaky Leg for tricking me with a rib.

czech

I was in college when I told my dad, "I'm going to be an actor." He didn't say anything; instead, every two weeks I would get these letters in the mail. Well, actually, they were newspaper clippings. Clippings with headlines like, "ACTOR STARVES TO DEATH IN NEW YORK." There was another one that read, "ONLY TWO PERCENT ACTORS' UNION EMPLOYED." And another one: "BOB CRANE, STAR OF HOGAN'S HEROES, FOUND STABBED TO DEATH." At the top of the article, in red pen, was the handwritten line "Georgette, send to Kevin." Georgette was the name of my dad's secretary. No return address, no written letter, just "Georgette, send to Kevin." At first I thought that was my dad's way of saying, "Don't get into the theater. I do not want my son in the arts." Later

I wondered if Dad knew more about being an artist than I thought. No one goes into the arts on purpose.

In 1987 I got a job with the Actors Theatre of Louisville. They were going to Czechoslovakia and would be the first American company to tour that country in fifteen years. They hired me not only as an actor but they also wanted me to perform one of my own plays. So I flew down to Louisville and we rehearsed for two weeks, and then one day they sat us down around a table in this huge room. We were all sitting there—the actors, the technicians, and the stage manager—and we were to be briefed by a member of the U.S. State Department. The INS. He was going to tell us the dos and don'ts of visiting a communist country.

This man walks in wearing a blue suit and a blue tie, and he slams his briefcase down and says, "We're not going to have another Moscow incident here, are we?"

"What?"

"We're not going to have another Moscow incident, where Sergeant Lonetree let those prostitutes into the American Embassy and they took photographs of our secret documents. We're *not* going to have another Moscow incident here, are we?"

And I'm thinking, "Jeez, we're a bunch of actors. What are we going to do, give away secrets on O'Neill?"

He says, "No drugs!" And he points right at me. "No drugs! I know about you actors!" And I'm thinking, "How does he know about the seventies?"

Then he points to the woman next to me. He says, "No fraternizing. No fraternizing—and I think you know what

I mean by fraternizing." His eyebrows are going up and down, yoing-yoing-yoing. I try to lean over into Fraternizing. *I* want to be a fraternizer.

"No drugs!" He shouts me back, "No drugs! And no illegal literature! Don't try to sneak in any Kafka. It's been banned."

No Kafka? What are we going to do for fun?

"And *you!*" he's pointing at me again. "*You* can't do your play," he said. "It's been banned in Czechoslovakia."

I'd been looking forward to doing my play. I've been banned? Wait a minute, I've been banned? Hey! I must've written something important. I've been banned! I've been banned!

Then the man said, "And I know you actors. There are no homosexuals in Czechoslovakia. No homosexuals in Czechoslovakia."

One of our company members is gay. When we all finally got to Czechoslovakia, we were there only ten minutes when he walked up the street, came back, and said, "Seven."

We get on this bus that would take us from Prague to Brno. I take a minute to read a pamphlet given to us by the INS. It's a booklet titled *Common Czech Phrases* and on the first page it says, "I'll have a pageboy haircut, please" and "This room smells of vermin."

Where are we going? We're on the road when all of a sudden, "BEE-DO-BEE-DO-BEE-DO." There's this official car behind us. So our bus pulls over and this official gets on. He says, "Does anyone speak Czech?" Nobody says anything but I know there are at least three people on the bus who speak Czech. He repeats, "Does anyone speak Czech?" Nothing. Finally he shouts, "WHO HERE SPEAKS CZECH?" And Michal Z. raises his hand.

Michal Z., our interpreter. I'll never forget seeing him for the first time—waiting in the Prague airport, chest out, wearing this leather jacket. Michal's standing there smoking a cigarette. Michal Z.

So Michal and the official get off the bus and I see them go to the official's car. They stand there—the official is talking and Michal's got this cigarette in his mouth . . . his hand shakes as he lights it. As it burns, the ashes drop down onto his shirt and pants. Then the official gets back into his car and leaves, and Michal gets back on the bus.

He comes back and sits down, and turns to me and says, "I'm a member of the Jazz Club."

I say, "What, you're in a band, you play an instrument?"

He says, "No, I am a member of the Jazz Club. We are a group of artists who are going to change the country. Václav Havel, the playwright, is our leader. You know who Václav Havel is?"

I didn't at the time.

Michal says, "He is in prison now. When he gets out, we will change this country."

WE ARRIVE IN BRNO and set up in a museum where the Actors Theatre of Louisville is performing. Michal was positioned with a microphone in this little glass booth behind the audience. As we acted onstage, he would translate what we said through the microphone—and through headsets to people sitting in the audience. He was a great interpreter. The place was packed. We sell out every show because on the first day we got a bad review in the communist paper. They just slammed us. People said, "Bad review, communist paper: got to be a good play!" Packed.

After the show one day, Michal said, "You have to come meet my friend Rostyov!" So we went to meet Rostyov in his little, tiny apartment. Big Rostyov, little apartment. We get inside and he's lined up these two long rows of shot glasses. He takes his Slivovitz, this plum brandy, and he pours the shot glasses full down one side. Then he pours the shot glasses full down the other side and hands me one. Michal takes a shot glass for himself and Rostyov says, "Each one of these is a soldier. Tonight we drink an army." And we start drinking through our respective armies.

After a while I say, "Rostyov! This is amazing. This is the strongest stuff I've ever had!"

He says, "You like it? I made it myself!"

"Ah!" I say, "Rostyov, you can go blind on homemade stuff!"

And he says, "Yes, but the store-bought stuff will kill you!"

Finally I had to quit. I say, "You guys, I can't keep up with you. I can't believe how much you can drink."

"Oh," they say, "we don't drink anything like the Poles. And they don't drink anything like the Russians."

And I'm thinking, "Oppression can sure put a liver on a man."

Rostyov told me the secret to handling great quantities of alchohol.

"Eat a lot of pork."

I say, "Rostyov, that's all there is to eat."

"Exactly," he says. Another soldier drops.

LATER THAT NIGHT I said to Michal, "You speak English so well. Better than I do. How come?" And he told me, "I studied in your country. I lived in your country, but they banned my work in Czechoslovakia. So I decided to move back here. Now they can make my life miserable, but they can't stop me from reaching my people."

I said, "Hey, I wrote a play that was banned here. I wrote this play and it was banned in Czechoslovakia."

And Rostyov said, "Then we have to do your play."

So we do my play in Czechoslovakia . . . underground. Michal invited all these members of the Jazz Club and I invited all the people from the Actors Theatre of Louisville. Michal was such a good interpreter that by the audience response you couldn't tell where the Americans were sitting or where the Czechs were sitting. The laughter would come at the same time. I remember watching him up in the booth. I'd see Michal gesturing wildly. And I thought, "Well, I gotta keep up with him." So I started gesturing wildly. Back and forth, back and forth, and finally at the end of the play, the audience didn't even applaud. Instead, they rushed the stage and we had this massive hug right there in the middle of the floor.

And that's when I remembered something the guy in the blue suit back in the States had said: "You will be followed. You *will* be followed." I looked around that massive hug and I wondered if somebody there had followed me and was now taking down names. I went back to my room and took the receiver off the phone and sure enough, there was a bug.

And that night when I went to bed, people's faces from the Jazz Club kept coming at me and I'd wake up in cold sweats.

And the next night I couldn't sleep at all and when I went to the museum, I thought, "Oh, good, that woman was at the play and she's here. Oh good, he's here." And I would start counting the heads of people I knew had been at the play. Counting their heads, then asking, "Where'd that guy go? Where's that guy?" And they'd say, "He's at lunch now." And I'd be a nervous wreck until he came back.

On most nights I couldn't sleep at all but every time I nodded off I'd wake up in these cold sweats again. Finally I thought, "Okay, that's it. I've got to do something about this."

So I went to the Embassy in Prague and I told the American ambassador: "Look, I did my play. I knew I wasn't supposed to. But I did my play and I put these people in jeopardy. What can I do about it?"

And he said, "Well, first of all, stop worrying about the Czechs. They didn't ban your play. We did."

"Why?"

He said, "We don't like the way your play portrays America."

WHEN I WAS in Brno every once in a while the Jazz Club would put on a performance, sometimes music, sometimes theater, but always in the middle of the night. To be associated with "unsanctioned" art could be costly. One could lose a job or an apartment or worse. So these events were kept quiet. One night we drove to a secluded spot in a forest to see a performance artist. He came highly recommended. We arrived at three in the morning to find a mound of dirt. Everyone turned their cars so the headlights illuminated the mound. Then we waited. At five past the hour a nervousness set in—because of the risk involved, nothing started late. At ten past, nervousness turned to panic. "Something has happened." "Go, go." "Let's get out of here." People scrambled for their cars and everyone sped away wondering what had befallen the performance artist. We learned the next day that he had been there. He was under the mound of dirt breathing through a straw. That was his piece.

Before I left Czechoslovakia I was approached by a man who worked at the theater. He said, "You have to get these pictures out. They're of the performance artist you saw." There were several pictures of the mound of dirt. I carefully rolled them up and wrapped them around my leg. I had other pieces of art wrapped around my other leg as well. My legs looked perfectly cylindrical, like the Tin Man from

Wizard of Oz. Somehow the angels were with me; at the airport, security men were frisking every third person and I was a two. I flew home a nervous wreck because I had a photo of a mound of dirt strapped to my leg.

I remembered something Michal had said to me before I left Czechoslovakia: "One day we will be free. It will be a large transition but we'll be fine. It's your country I worry about. As long as there is communism you have some place to put your fears. When we change you'll have no more place. Your fears will then come home."

Communism fell in the Czech Republic in 1989. Michal had said that after they elected a Polish pope it was just a matter of time. However, the artists were at the forefront of the final push. The Czechs hold the arts close to their hearts. It has been a tonic and a hope in desperate times. In the market I remember the only line longer than the one for bananas was the one for new books. The first people to stop performing were from the symphony and they were followed by the theater performers. They all announced that their next performance would only be for a free country. Then the people joined in what is now called the "Velvet Revolution."

In 1989 the wall separating East from West came down. That same year the U.S. Congress added the anti-obscenity clause to all funding from the National Endowment for the Arts. The fear had come home.

fear

Fear as a child is absolute and immediate, it's life and death, it's black and white—not like fear as an adult, which is gray and goes on all the time. This is a story about fear as a child.

Recess. Mrs. Jensen's fifth-grade class. I'm behind the brick pump house where my 35 cents of lunch money has just bought a viewing of Mary Gilligan's appendix scar. All of a sudden my best friend, Earl, rounds the corner with the look of terror that only a kid with red hair and white eyebrows can get. He's screaming, "We're dead men!" Stomping on the end of his shadow, brandishing two baseball bats, is a girl named Katie. As I turned to run, I feel the impact of the bat against the back of my head. I feel a cold wave rush forward and a low hum in my ears, and a blue-black tunnel forms around my vision; the light at the end gets smaller and smaller and then I pass out.

The next day Mr. Felber, the principal, announced that bats were to remain off the playground for an indefinite period of time. The last indefinite period of time was six months when a kid named Mike got hit in the head with a bat while playing baseball. Everyone said Mike was never the same after that when, in fact, he was the same after that clear into adulthood. When I came to, the doctor told me I had a concussion but would be OK. When I got back to school Mr. Felber announced it was nice to have me back. But I looked around the room and I knew it was my fault that there were no more bats on the playground and it did not feel so nice to have me back.

First up for show-and-tell Katie did a slide show presentation of her brother in Vietnam. She also read a letter he sent that was full of words that were "off-color" according to Mrs. Jensen, but Katie was allowed to continue. In her brother's letter he said it was so hot in Vietnam you could fry an egg on a rock, and sure enough in one of the slides Katie's brother was with a buddy, frying an egg on a rock.

Just then Earl turned around his little robin egg–blue eyeballs, looking back at me, and I could tell he wanted to laugh. When your best friend wants to laugh you want to laugh— law of nature—but this was not a good time so I suppressed it. But the laugh went searching for a weak gasket and finally found it in my nose. "Hank." The whole class turned around.

"Hank." Mrs. Jensen yelled "Boys!" and I looked up. Katie was staring at me, memorizing me for later.

After show-and-tell we're in the hallway putting on our rubber shoes for gym class. I looked down the row of lockers and saw Katie's open locker and inside were hanging two baseball bats. She looks at me and smiles. In gym class we play "Bombardment," a game where you throw stinky rubber balls at other children as hard you can. It's part of the Presidential Fitness Plan. Now in Bombardment Katie could have hit me a million times but instead she stops and throws at other kids, obviously saving me "for later." After gym I was waiting my turn to use the boy's room. I knew it was going to happen on the playground and I started to imagine the feeling of the baseball bat hitting the back of my head. I started to feel the cold wave and blue-black and humming and then I got a waft from the cafeteria and . . . fish sticks, it must be Friday. I threw up. In no time the janitor was there with the green sawdust. Swoop and he was gone. Earl said, "I'll take Kevin to the nurse's office" and on the way he said, "You can't go home."

"What do you mean?" I asked.

You throw up. You go home. It's automatic.

"You go home and I am a dead man," Earl said.

So I talk the nurse out of sending me home.

She said, "Are you sure?"

Earl said, "Yes, he's sure."

We went back to the room. Katie couldn't believe it either. She looked at me and smiled.

Recess. I'm hiding behind the pump house; Mary Gilligan can have her scar. Sure enough around the corner comes Earl with that look of terror and "we're dead men!" I burst into the flat and split off, trying to confuse Katie. I look back and she's following me. Then I remember Mutual of Omaha's *Wild Kingdom:* the cheetah follows the weak and the sick. My only hope is the giant slide, and I gather up all my speed and approach from the slick part of the slide. 1234567. 677. 6. 7. I grab onto the top of the slide and pull myself up, and I'm safe. If Katie goes up the slick part I'll climb down the ladder. If is she climbs up the ladder, I'll slide down the slick part. It is a cycle that can go all recess long. I stand on top of the slide as Katie hovers below. And that's when I see the Foshay Tower, the thirty-two-story building in downtown Minneapolis. Tallest building from Chicago to San Francisco. Tallest building there will ever be. If I live to the sixth grade I'll go see it on a field trip.

I yell down, "Katie, I can see the Foshay Tower," and she believes me and climbs up the ladder. I slide down the slick part and look up to watch her with two bats in her hands. She's yelling, "I discovered the Foshay Tower."

Later that night Earl and I are walking home. We know we're safe because Katie is now Queen of the Playground.

YEARS LATER I'm sitting on the roof of Earl's house. We can see the Foshay Tower in the distance. We're putting new shingles on his roof and Earl is yelling to his sister below: "Look out down there, we're throwing shingles." We're talking tough because we've just been issued draft cards for Vietnam. This is a rite of passage that lets you talk tough to hide the fear. Suddenly Earl turns to me and says, "Do you still have a cabin up north?"

I said, "Yes."

He said, "Can you sneak me into Canada?"

And then I imagine Earl in Vietnam with his red hair and white eyebrows. I knew I'd never have to go. My body was not acceptable. I could afford to talk tough. Finally I said "Earl, it really would be frightening to go to Vietnam."

"That's not why," he said. "I'm not afraid. Do you remember Katie's brother?"

"I don't think he ever came back," I said.

"I don't think he did either," he said. "Do you remember what that did to her? Remember what that did to Katie? I'm not doing that to my sister."

So I snuck Earl into Canada. We were standing on a Canadian highway. His thumb was out, mine was not.

I said, "Earl, I don't know when I'll see you again."

He said, "Yes you do. I can't go through with it."

So I snuck Earl back into Minnesota.

I don't know what was said between him and the government but they decided he would go to Idaho and, with a team of seven mules, mark trails in the mountains.

It was supposedly a horrible job, but Earl loved it. I haven't seen him since and last I heard it's what he does to this day. But I think of him a lot, and the time I watched his fear shift from black and white to gray.

"dick"

Part of everyday life when you're disabled is frustration. Sometimes living with a disability becomes more than I can handle. The best advice I can give is find an advocate, someone who can think clearly and speak for you in your time of need. Remember: the squeaky wheel gets the grease. You need to be relentless and persistent, especially when dealing with the medical industry. I have a buddy who is a lawyer and he used to represent people in lawsuits against the big health care companies. Now he's working for renewable energy. He fights oil companies because he feels it's a battle he can actually win.

If you don't have a person develop a persona. An alter ego. I found mine in a classic character from literature.

When I was a kid my mom read me the fairy tale about the ugly duckling. It's where this huge, geeky duck can't fit in with the other ducks. He steps on them and breaks everything until finally he finds out he's really a beautiful swan. I liked it better when he thought he was a duck. A huge über duck that was large and superior to the other ducks. But it turns out he's a swan like all the other swans, not a duck. What does that do for me, a disabled kid? Hope a ship of aliens lands who all look like me and say, "Hey, you're really one of us"? Meanwhile, I'm stuck living with the ducks.

Fairy tales usually end up bad for the disabled guy. Snow White trades in seven perfectly good small guys for one big handsome one. Rumpelstiltskin actually grabs one leg at the end of his story and rips himself asunder. (Alright, I kind of like that one.)

In the seventies there were cop shows. Every demographic had a cop.

Inner city had Shaft.

Trailer parks had Rockford.

Tropical paradise had Steve McGarrett.

Teenagers had the Mod Squad.

Bald Greeks had Kojak.

Everyone had Angie Dickinson.

We had Ironside. Dang. Ironside was named after a battleship. Now I always liked Raymond Burr—he was like a poor man's Lee J. Cobb. But I wanted my cop in a Lamborghini, not a van. I wanted chicks to swoon for him. And those other shows had the same soundtrack: "Waka waka waka." It was designed for running and shooting, not rolling and delegating.

But then I saw Ian McKellen play Shakespeare's King Richard the Third and I thought, there's my man. Granted he was played by an able-bodied actor, which to me was like watching a white guy play Othello. And then he did a bit where he put on a glove with one hand that sent the audience into hysterics. I thought, man, if this place saw me put on my socks there wouldn't be a dry seat in the house. But I thought he did a good job for an able-bodied guy.

His ruthlessness was fun to watch. It was easy to cheer for him. He killed the handsome guy then took his girl.

I loved Richard. I knew others feared and despised him, but it's a matter of perspective. Look: the only difference between an annoying dripping faucet and a peaceful Japanese fountain is perspective.

Still leaking water.

So this was my man. My alter ego. But I wanted my Richard from Minnesota, up near the Iron Range where they grow 'em tough, so I called him "Dick da Tird." My main trouble with Richard is that he never felt love. The whole reason Richard the Third gives for his revenge is that no one will love him.

> But I, that am not shap'd for sportive tricks,
> Nor made to court an amorous looking-glass;
> I, that am rudely stamp'd, and want love's majesty

To strut before a wanton ambling nymph;
I that am curtail'd of this fair proportion,
Cheated of feature by dissembling nature,
Deform'd, unfinish'd, sent before my time
Into this breathing world, scarce half made up . . .
    And therefore, since I cannot prove a lover,
To entertain these fair well-spoken days,
I am determined to prove a villain . . .

He says it right off the bat—since he can't find love, it's better to be a villain than be ignored. It's true. Disliked is better than to disappear.

In Mary Shelley's tale, Frankenstein's creature tries to get a mate the conventional way, but he keeps accidentally killing people. Like Lenny in *Of Mice and Men*, he simply pets too hard. So the monster asks his creator Dr. Frankenstein to make a creature like himself, someone to love. Now Dr. Frankenstein learns the dilemma of creation. When you've created a monster how do you stop? Shelley wrote this book when she was nineteen. How did she know so much about guys? That's what's scary.

But I understand it. People want to fit in to be loved. Except for Richard.

My favorite ending to a tale is in *The Hunchback of Notre Dame*. It starts with the description of the cemetery and goes like this.

By the end of the fifteenth century, this formidable gibbet

. . . had fallen upon evil days. The beams were worm-eaten,
the chains corroded with rust, the pillars green with mould,
the blocks of hewn stone gaped away from one another, and
grass was growing on that platform on which no human
foot ever trod now. The structure showed a ghastly silhou-
ette against the sky—especially at night, when the moon-
light gleamed on whitened skulls, and the evening breeze,
sweeping through the chains and skeletons, set them all rat-
tling in the gloom. . . . To that deep charnel-house, where so
many human remains and the memory of so many crimes
have rotted and mingled together, many a great one of the
earth, and many an innocent victim have contributed their
bones. . . (Victor Marie Hugo, *Notre Dame of Paris*, 1917).

As for the mysterious disappearance of Quasimodo, this
is all that we have been able to discover.

About a year and a half or two years after the concluding
events of this story . . . there were found among all those
hideous carcasses two skeletons, the one clasped in the
arms of the other. One of these skeletons . . . was that of a
woman. . . . The other skeleton, which held this so close a
clasp, was that of a man. It was observed that the spine was
crooked, the skull compressed between the shoulder-blades,
and that one leg was shorter than the other. There was
no rupture of the vertebrae at the nape of the neck, from
which it was evident that the man had not been hanged. He
must, therefore, have come of himself and died there. When

they attemped to detach this skeleton from the one it was embracing, it fell to dust.

There we are, the grotesque grabbing onto beauty, beauty embraced by the grotesque, the light surrounded by the shadow. Our lives rounded by a little sleep.

perception

I've been in a lot of hospital waiting rooms over the last years, waiting for x-rays, waiting for tests. The usual emergency room wait is about three to four hours. Every time an ambulance shows up add on another hour because they tend to go to the head of the line. Sometimes whatever I was in there for quits doing what it was doing before I can see a doctor, so I just go home.

Waiting rooms are very different, depending on what part of the country you're in. Up north they're really quiet. Northerners are very private about their pain. They disapprove of being a "show-off," of that unappealing quality associated with attention-drawing sound or movement, even when it's from pain. When I was down south in a Virginia waiting room, people were telling everyone else their whole life stories. On and on they went. One woman talked about her foot and her gall bladder and that they are still finding shards in her head, and she wasn't even there to see a doctor—she'd brought her friend in.

As I watched her I completely forgot I was in pain. It's amazing how distraction can relieve pain. I went to a website that talks about chronic pain and one constant in all of pain management is the use of distraction.

It's true. I'm in a theater company called Interact and most of our actors are disabled, but whenever we're on stage our disjointed twists and turns ease out a bit. I've never been in pain while I've been performing; I wish I could say the same for the audience.

According to one Greek story, when the god Hephaestus was born his mother Hera didn't like what she saw so she threw him off Mount Olympus. Hephaestus dragged his broken form to Hades and started to work, forging metal into beautiful objects: Eros's bow and arrows, Helios's chariot, and Hermes' winged helmet and sandals.

From what I can tell Hephaestus, the disabled god, was the only god that actually held down a job. I think that's why Aphrodite, the most beautiful goddess of all, married him. He had a job. She knew what she was doing. But Hephaestus's work went beyond usefulness. He had used his craft to take him out of hell. A job will do that.

Perception.

There's a folktale about a man who goes to town for

supplies and finds a mirror. He has never seen a mirror before. He looks in it and thinks he sees a picture of his father. He brings the mirror home and later his wife finds it hidden under the bed. She looks in it and sees a woman. Obviously, the woman thinks her husband is having an affair with another woman in town. This woman looks just like the kind of hussy her husband would fall for, too. A huge fight breaks out and a frying pan is involved and finally the husband and wife discover the mirror is a looking glass. Ahhh, now they're in love again and she gets a bag of ice for his head.

Mirrors are deceiving. When it comes right down to it, we don't believe what we see; rather, we see what we *believe*. Just like the couple in the folktale, we see what we want to see. Sometimes you look in the mirror and think, "Oh no! I look like that?" But when you look in a mirror and your love looks over and says, "You're hot," you're hot. And it's true . . . you *are* hot. Same mirror.

One time I was in New York. I walked out onto the street and saw a bike messenger run into a woman. He was going pretty fast and she was screaming, "Get away, get away!" I saw the whole thing and, even though she was hit hard, I thought she took the blow pretty well and would be OK. I calmly approached her and she stopped screaming. I said I'd seen the whole thing and she'd be fine. "Lay still and the ambulance will be here," I told her. She said thank you and calmly waited. People were looking at me with appreciation. And I was thinking just approach a situation calmly and everything will be fine. I was feeling pretty good about myself when I looked down and noticed I was wearing a blue hospital shirt, a top scrub like doctors wear that I'd bought at a thrift store. That poor woman thought I was a doctor. Oh well. It worked.

AT MY BROTHER'S wedding there was a waltz playing and I knew that my grandmother wanted to dance. "Grandmother, would you like to dance?" I asked.

We got up and we started to move and I'm doing a terrible job. But then I remembered something my Uncle Johnny taught me. Uncle Johnny, the best dancer in our family, used to say, "Cinch 'em in, Kev. Just cinch 'em in." So I cinched Grandmother in and we got smoother and smoother and pretty soon we were moving pretty good. I was dancing for the first time in my life. With my grandmother! I wanted to see that look in her eye, you know, that look that says, "We're really cutting up the rug." So I glanced over to get that look but her eyes were closed and she was smiling. I don't know who she was dancing with, but it sure wasn't me.

PERCEPTION, deception, refraction, distraction.

We see it when we believe it.

We are all so worried about being deceived. Take a day off. Stand in front of a mirror and have your loved one tell you how great you look. Believe me, you look hot.

australia

I'm in Perth, Australia. I'm as far away from Minnesota
as you can get and still be on dry land. I'm there watching
the America's Cup, a boat race where Dennis Connor, the
American, is trying to win back the trophy he lost to the
Australians four years ago. I love this sport because it happens so far out in the ocean you can't see it, so you stay in
the bar and drink until someone comes in and tells you
who won.

This event, like all good hosts, doesn't interfere with
the party. And Perth is wild—"Waltzing Matilda" twenty-
four hours a day, pubs packed with tourists. There is this
woman standing on top of a cigarette machine, waving a
large American flag, and as she passes the flag over the

Australians' heads, they try to light it with their Bic lighters. But it won't burn. They can't get it to burn.

After this race I ask the Australians, "What's fun to do here? What's fun in Australia?"

"You've got to see the rock, mate. You've got to climb the rock. You haven't been to Australia until you've climbed Ayers Rock."

So the next morning I get on a jet and fly to the middle of the great arid continent of Australia, and I get off at Alice Springs. Then I get on a smaller plane, a little one-prop job like my dad's, and we fly to this landing strip in the middle of the outback and get on a bus. We drive with our windows open and the heat and the dirt are blowing in from the outside. When we stop the Americans smoke and the Japanese take pictures. We load back up. Sitting next to me is this guy from Holland. His name is Arnie Tang and he's singing in this heavy accent, "Der wus a hoose in Neoorlins, dey call de risin' sun." He's got this beat-up guitar that he says, "I am being carrying all over de wurld." Arnie talks just like a neon sign I read in Amsterdam once. It said, "Real f***ing live show!!!" I still don't know what that meant, and Arnie had the same quality. "It wus de ruin of many a man und Gott I hope I'm one."

Finally, I see Ayers Rock on the horizon. This guy, a tourist guide, gets on the loudspeaker:

"G'day mates (*static*), and welcome to Ayers Rock, the world's largest monolith. I know you've all come to climb the rock but before you do, I'd like to remind you that two hundred and fifteen people have died from heart attacks and another fifty have dropped to their impending death. Enjoy your stay and enjoy the rock (*click*)."

Arnie says, "But I have been coming to climb the rock."

And I say, "I am coming to climb the rock."

He says, "Well, I am climbing the rock."

I say, "I am climbing the rock."

People get off the bus and are cutting the rock a wide berth. Arnie and I walk right up to the base of the rock, grab this chain that's hanging down the side, and start pulling ourselves up to the top. I wanted to quit three times, and about halfway up I say, "Arnie, I don't think I'm going to make it."

Arnie says, "I am keeping going."

So I say, "I am keeping going, too!"

We get to the top, then we grab that chain and let ourselves back down, trying not to become statistics.

That night we're at the campground. I could see Ayers Rock in the distance and I'm standing there doing the Australian salute, which is a hand wave in front of your face to keep the flies away, and behind me the sun is setting. As the red from the sun hit that rock, it starts to glow this brilliant red. Then as the sun sets further, that rock turns into this deep, blood red. As the coolness of the night hit the heat of that rock, it starts to move and to beat. The sun set, but I know out there in the darkness the heart of Australia is still beating. I go back to my tent and I write in my journal, "*No atheist leaves the rock.*"

■ ■ ■

DAVID IS A BARRISTER—a lawyer—for the Aboriginal land rights in Alice Springs. I met him shortly after my visit to the rock. David explains that recently the United States, more accurately the CIA, was buying land in the outback. David has been helping native people here acquire their land through the court system, but records are sparse and inconsistent.

David goes inside and comes back wearing his powder wig and his black robe that his grandfather had used back in England. He's standing there in the 110 degree heat, sweat running from under the wig, and he said, "The first people here didn't understand this. And we certainly didn't understand them. There are hundreds of native languages in Australia but not one word for 'possession' or 'time'. My job is all the more difficult because there is also a different sense of family."

I say, "Wait a second there, David. Family . . . that seems kind of cut-and-dried to me."

He says, "No, our system, the Western system, runs vertically, like a family tree. That means your great-grandparents, your grandparents, your parents going up the trunk and your uncles and cousins going out on the branches . . . your vertical tree. But their family tree is like vines running horizontally around the earth." Although a matriarchal system, a "brother," for instance, may be the son of your mother's sister; you're also associated with a living creature, a totem, or dreaming.

Part of one's heritage is also a stewardship of the land. For this reason Australia has many sacred sites. One is Uluru, or what white fellas call Ayers Rock. I told David I'd climbed the rock. His look said, "I wish you hadn't done that."

All of a sudden I wished I hadn't either.

When David told me that Uluru was a sacred site, it bothered me that I had climbed it. It still bothers me to this day. The sacred isn't something to be conquered. By accepting and knowing that it is sacred, we show respect. By showing respect we are rewarded at times by glimpses into those worlds that lay beyond our grasp. I feel extremely fortunate that the rock chose to show me a bit of its power that night at the campsite. Even though I had crossed a boundary, there remained an invitation, a bit of unfinished business. As Dante learned, to reach his Beatrice in Paradise he would first need to experience the Inferno. I would as well—this time and again—enter the sacred through the profane.

my brother's
bachelor party

My brother is getting married, so his pals and I decided
to throw a bachelor party. We convene at the bowling alley
for an intensive planning session. At first the thoughts are
simple and heartfelt, a few close friends, some cigars, a fine
peppermint schnapps perhaps, but in a relatively short period of time we are huddled around a ballpoint pen and a
map of Minneapolis, charting a downtown tour of Mephis-
tophelian proportions. Over the din of shattering pins, one
of the more lucid voices cries, "We should make a day of it.
I know where we can get a school bus."

On the morning of the big day we reconvene. There is

an enthusiasm in the air—something is going to happen today, something certainly to retell and embellish time and again during cold evenings at the pub. These are the moments one feels the tingle that he is about to do something he ought to know better than, perhaps requiring stitches.

As we await the guest of honor, one of our members, who answers to the title "Lumper," dashes from his automobile, pale and breathless. He relates that my brother is presently recovering at the hospital, after receiving a horrific dog bite. A dog bite. I recall with horror, my own brush with a cur that went by the breed Weimaraner. A hoary beast, without provocation or warning, lunged at me from behind a shrub. I felt the tinge of brutish teeth lodge in my calf. I have since learned this specific breed of dog, Weimaraner, was developed in nineteenth-century Germany, as a hunting companion, more specifically to bring down male deer by their genitalia. I now regard my brush as rather fortunate, accounts all taken, and have avoided the breed with the respect due its purpose. But my brother, good God, a dog bite.

"Where? How? What dog?"

"His own dog," replied Lumper.

His dog. My brother's dog is a happy, slobbering Springer Spaniel. Wouldn't hurt a fly if it were wearing a bacon jacket and slacks.

"No, his dog was in a scrap with another dog. When Steven tried to separate the combatants, his dog, thinking it was the throat of the other dog, bit his ankle, leaving a healthy gash requiring eight to twelve stitches at last count."

A feasible explanation. While his dog was friend to all men, the creature held a great contempt for his own species, a fault I fear of premature weaning and a neglect of early socialization. We can learn much from the animal kingdom.

"Quick man, what hospital?"

We loaded into our *charabanc* and proceeded toward the hospital. We find my brother patched and paid for and pleased that his chums were all frothed in the matter of his immediate release.

We head to Hubert H. Humphrey Metrodome baseball arena. The boys amuse themselves in the back of the bus with a rousing game of "Does this hurt more, or less?" We take our assigned seats and discover we have been placed quite a distance from the center of the action. Some of the lads have brought their baseball-catching gloves, in hopes of snagging an errant home run. The banner marking "The furthest ball ever hit in the dome" is some fifteen rows in front of us. The likelihood of a free souvenir appears rather nil. This does nothing to douse our enthusiasm. Quite the contrary, we shout and cheer. We have come to have fun, by heavens, and brought plenty of our own friends so as not to be under any obligation to make new ones. Our enthusiasm is quickly met with a brace of barrel-chested ushers. We all put on our best behavior, and settle into a meal of tubular cuisine *mitt kraut*.

The Twins baseball match has hit a dull stretch. Also, our morning imbibing has worn off and we have "turned the corner," transforming us into a rather surly collection of revelers. We're bored, and when my brother is bored, no amount of beefed-up security is going to prevent something from happening.

Suddenly he says, "You see that kid?" He points several rows down where perches a twosome of adolescent boys, greedily helping themselves to a variety of unhealthy, complexion-ravaging foodstuffs.

"Five bucks says when that kid is done with his nachos, he licks his cheese compartment."

A wager! Money immediately makes its way out of pockets.

"Yeah, I'm in for five."

"Yeah, me too."

Lumper intercedes, "Now, does he have to lick the compartments or can he clean it out with his finger and lick that?"

"No," my brother announces. "He will put his tongue in the actual compartment itself."

Lumper is in for five. Jay McBroom wants to know if the kid has to finish all the cheese that remains.

"No," says my brother, "one lick."

Jay McBroom adds his five to the growing pile. A gentleman behind us explains he couldn't help overhearing our wager and wonders if he can get a piece of the action.

"Of course," says my brother.

His companion considers himself an expert on human nature.

"That young man was raised too well. Simply look at his attire. You have it all wrong to believe he would stoop to such crassness."

His theory is heartily met with, "Put your money where your mouth is, pal."

"Okay, but can he use his finger to . . ."

"No."

"Alright, I'm in."

And so is the gentleman next to him. Then, like a fire at the gauze works, one can see the bet spread through the stands. It travels up and over the portals, around pillars, over to the next section, and to the next. The ushers sense something is amiss. They alertly employ a walkie-talkie and request back-up. More ushers arrive and take their stations. Too late, the betting continues to spread. High above us and to the right I can see a man take out his money, point to the kid, then mime the licking of the compartment to his neighbor. The neighbor reaches into his pocket. Somewhere across the field a section cheers. We all lean in fast and look at the kid. Was it a premature lick? No, it was only the Twins scoring the go-ahead run. We are led to understand it was a terrific play. Someone starts to explain it.

"Shut up."

For we have arrived at the moment of truth. The unsuspecting child has finished his last nacho. There is not a peep. I can hear a cricket in the bleachers as everyone leans in, all eyes focused on the nacho container and the child of destiny.

"Come on," a man blurts.

"Shhhhh, you'll spook him."

I hear whispering. "Lick it."

"Don't lick it."

"Lick it."

"Don't lick it."

"For God's sake, lick it."

"Come on, lick it you little . . ."

"Come on, come on, please, oh please."

"Shut up."

"You shut up."

The kid looks left, and then he looks right. And as the child of fortune tongues that cheese compartment, a cheer erupts the likes of which I've never heard before or since at the Dome. The entire outfield section began yelling as one: loud, raucous, and insane. The members of both baseball squads turn and face our party, our party that is now in a destructive frenzy and under assault by a goon squad of strong-armed ushers. We will pay heavily for this outburst, but for that brief moment in time the Minnesota Twins are watching us. It is the ecstasy. Then, as God is my witness, Kirby Puckett, center fielder and future member of America's Baseball Hall of Fame, smiles at our merry band and doffs his cap. I love Minnesota.

if it's morphine
it must be august

I'm sitting in the coffee shop slowing digging out bus change and laying it carefully on the table. It's a strange-looking ritual, but ever since my motorcycle accident, my right arm is paralyzed and my other has always had a congenital condition. It is much shorter, a bit crooked, with no thumb, so now my arms work like Lenny and George from *Of Mice and Men*. One can't catch the rabbits; the other can't seem to remember the rabbits. It takes all of my concentration to manipulate both a dollar and a quarter so when the bus comes I can spring into action.

As careful as I am, a quarter falls on the floor. If I could take off my shoe and sock I could get it. My feet have become downright prehensile over the past few months, not that I can deal a round of blackjack, and I understand if you don't want me to open your can of Sprite, but I could get this quarter. What is proper etiquette here? I feel my head getting hot. The people around me are beautiful and healthy, smoking and flirting, and this fuels my frustration.

"I, that am rudely stamp'd," like Shakespeare's King Richard the Third says. "Unfinish'd, sent before my time into this breathing world scarce half made up; . . . since I cannot prove a lover to entertain these fair well-spoken days, I am determined to [be] a villain." In other words, sometimes I just lose it. But not today; I let the quarter go.

A lot of the folks around me are tattooed and pierced. I think about getting a tattoo to hide some of my recent scars, maybe a flowered vine that uses the scar as a trellis, or a snake. Finally, I decide I want to get one that says in Gothic letters, "My other body is a weightlifter."

The scars are there because I've had a couple of surgeries to fix my brachial plexus. Brachial plexus is the confluence of nerves that connect the spine to the arm. Mine have been pulled out of the spine like a plug out of a socket. Unfortunately, doctors don't know how to plug them back in, but what can be done is nerves that are already plugged in can be rerouted to the troubled area. In my case, it's taking nerves from the rib area and redirecting them to the bicep and shoulder; or like my mechanic would say, "Robbing Peter to pay Paul." Peter is sensory nerves and Paul is motor nerves, and I pray Peter doesn't deny me, and Paul establishes a strong foundation. But you never know what will happen. When my dad used speaker cords to rewire the garage door opener I remember we ended up parking the car on the street a lot.

I read about one guy for months after his surgery who, every time he sneezed, raised his hand. I've got some time to find out what happens. Nerves grow at about an inch a month, so it will be a year or two before I know if the surgery worked. And I have at least one more surgery to go.

Each surgery lasts from eighteen to twenty-four hours. These are extremely focused hours, so these surgeons are like the Navy Seals of their profession. After being under the anesthesia so long, I come out talking like an old Walter Brennan for about three weeks. I then graduate to a young Walter Brennan, then to a Walter Brennan-type, to finally sounding like myself. I watch a lot of nature shows and cooking shows on television. I swear there's not a white shark in the ocean I don't know by sight. In fact, when I was watching *Iron Chef* the other day, a cooking show from Japan, I thought I recognized some of the ingredients.

During this time people stop by, friends who have cooked a meal. Sometimes people bring their kids by for a visit, but I know they're in the car afterward saying, "See what'll happen if you get a motorcycle."

Before the accident everyone had a story about a friend killed or maimed on a motorcycle. After the accident those stories disappear and are replaced with "Yeah, I knew a guy who hit a semi at eighty-five, flew three hundred feet, not a scratch, walked away and became a millionaire." I figure people need to tell these tales. It fights off the dread. If you know somebody it happened to, it lessons the chance it'll happen to you.

One time a kid came up to me and said, "I hit my head on a fence post and had to get eight stitches here." He points to the back of his head.

I said, "I have stitches," I start at one side of my head, "from here," I go around my head, down my side to below my stomach, "to here."

The kid pauses, "Yeah," he says, "but mine really hurt." He's got me there. There's no way to judge another man's pain.

These days I've got voice-activated software, which is a godsend. My computer reacts entirely on voice commands. It did take a while to get to know me. The first time I said, "Hello, my name is Kevin," it wrote, "The dog went to the store." Now we're getting along much better and often it writes better sentences than I command.

I use a lot of Velcro now. With Velcro everything sticks to everything. Velcro is as indiscriminate as the world's oldest profession, but is a lifesaver for closing up the gaps.

The worst part of this experience is the pain. Just because my arm doesn't work, doesn't mean there isn't any pain. In the description of my injury I read, "Pain is both ever-present and intermittent." At first this didn't make sense but now it does: it hurts unless it really hurts.

When nerves are damaged they continually register

"something is wrong"; the brain interprets this as pain. I've tried lots of homeopathic remedies for the pain: qigong, acupuncture, Reiki, and most of it works. One healer used golden pens, like ballpoint pens. They worked great. I asked him what they were. He told me they were some kind of hexagons with powder inside. Whatever, it works.

Some healers say that my accident is karma, atonement for past life actions. One woman said she would love to do a past life regression on me. "Man," she said, "you must've been bad." I turned her down. I don't want to know; if I am atoning for fun I had centuries ago it is probably best that I don't remember, kind of like college.

Before I had surgery I asked one healer if she thought I could fix the problem myself, through meditation. She said she believed one could grow back a severed arm. She said, "But it takes a master. I'm not a master, are you?" I decided to have surgery.

Whatever happens I do believe everything has its reason even though I'm not sure on which side of calamity the reason sits. It's true I'm learning a lot. This is a gift, but it's not one of those gifts I would have chosen for myself. Nothing is boring anymore. I get angry at heartless actions. It takes very little to make me cry. It feels good, although the anesthesia burns a bit as it cries out in my tears. Most of all, I don't want to become Richard the Third, but I can see how it happens.

Back in the coffee shop I dig out another quarter and head to the bus stop.

prayer

When I was a kid, I prayed to get things. I remember there was a squirrel monkey for sale in the back of *Spider-Man* comics for $9.99. I wanted that squirrel monkey. And not sea monkeys. Sea monkeys are a rip-off. Squirrel monkey. So I prayed to God to ask Jesus to tell Santa about that squirrel monkey, hoping with all my heart that one of the three would take my case.

Later in life, my prayers shifted. I'm on the Mediterranean Sea, on a boat between Athens, Greece, and the island of Ios, hanging on to a ladder for dear life. I stowed away. I stowed away because while on Ios, I discovered I only had $25 and I still wanted to see Italy and Ireland. So I bought a fake ticket for a dollar and got on board.

Once out to sea, I sat down next to a French guy, and I told him, "Hey, man, I stowed away."

He said, "You are in big trouble. They haven't even collected the tickets yet. When they find you, they are going to take you below." He said, "This happened to a friend of mine. They beat him with a bar of soap and a sock because it didn't show the bruises."

I gave the typical reply: "No they won't. I'm an American."

He said, "They're going to love you." And sure enough, an hour later, ticket-takers came, and I knew I was busted. So I hid behind these barrel-like, depth-charged things. But a steward saw my shoes and blew a whistle. It was cat-and-mouse around the ship. Then I see the ladder hanging over the side. I climb down the side and I'm hanging on over the water looking for any land I can swim to, and I prayed for the first time—for the first time in years I said, "God, please get me out of this. Get me out of this and I'll never do anything this stupid again as long as I live."

And I'm wild Russian boar hunting in Texas. Wild Russian boar were introduced to Texas for big-game hunting. They weigh five-, six-hundred pounds with six-inch tusks, and they eat meat in the middle of the night, which is you. So when they come to eat you in the night, you shoot them.

I'm what's called the light man. I hold a flashlight and search for a boar. I asked the guide Mario, "Mario, aren't they going to come for the guy with the light?" He says, "Yeah." So I decided right then and there if I see a boar, I'm going to shine the light on Mario. "Hoo—there's a big one."

Mario decides it's a good time to drink really a lot of Jack Daniels right out of the bottle. And then he decides to play this game called "Scare the Yankee." Mario has a license plate on his truck that reads, "My wife yes, my dog maybe, my gun . . . never." He takes out his Bowie knife and starts sliding it up my leg, showing me how it's going to feel when a boar gores me. All of a sudden, we look up and there's a cow standing there, a cow. Mario says: "My property, my cow." He takes out his six-shooter and blam, blam, blam, blam, blam, blam.

The cow looks at Mario, turns, and walks away. Oh, great. I'm the light man. Mario finishes the bottle and topples over, laying there out cold, on top of his gun. I'm standing there in the dark, waiting for a boar, and I pray to God, "God, please get me out of this. Get me out of this and I'll never do anything stupid again as long as I live." And I'm in Mardi Gras. Alright, you get the idea.

Five years ago, I'm in a motorcycle accident and my prayers changed yet again. I remember walking down the hall from rehab. I've been through many surgeries. And I'm in the hospital, a little over six weeks. And each day, I would ride the elevator to the ground floor and try to take a walk. I could go maybe half a block, but it felt really good to be in the sun. 9/11 had happened the week before. And as our country was entering trauma, I was living one. I already knew that you can't cure trauma. But hopefully, in time, you can heal from it. But it does take time.

I was on the elevator when I saw this guy who'd been

in the trauma ward when I was. I couldn't believe he was there and walking. When he arrived, he was barely alive—internal injuries, all four limbs in traction. And now, there he was, making his way into the sunshine. I wondered how he found the strength, so I asked, "How did you do it? You were even worse than I was." And he said, "Because they don't let you smoke in a hospital." And true to his word, when we got outside, he pounded a heater.

After my walk, my girlfriend Mary and I went into the gift shop, and she asked if I wanted an apple. She said they looked really good. Now, I hadn't tasted food in over a month and I had no taste. I lost a lot of weight because food had no appeal. So I said "No," but she persisted. "Come on. Try it." So finally, I said, "Alright." And I took a bite. And for some reason, that was the day flavor returned, and that powerful sweetness rushed from that apple. Oh, it was incredible.

I started to cry, cry for the first time in years. The tears flowed and as the anesthesia and antibiotics flushed through my tears, it burned my eyes. And between the sweetness of that apple and the burning of my tears, it felt so good to be alive. I blurted out, "thank you, thank you, thank you, thank you for this life." And that's when my prayers shifted, again, to giving thanks. And I don't know whether good things happen more because I was saying thank you, or I was just noticing them more.

But blessings started to emerge from the curses. For one thing, I get to see people at their best every day. Sometimes

I need help. And people are incredible, literally right there to lend a hand. And nobody looks better than when they're helping someone. And now when I pray, I take a moment to remind God to ask Jesus to tell Santa, if there's one thing I want, it's to say thank you, thank you, thank you—or a squirrel monkey.

the gift

In "A Child's Christmas in Wales," Dylan Thomas said that he can't remember whether he was six and it snowed for twelve days or he was twelve and it snowed for six. I know the feeling. Often when I ask memory to serve me, it doesn't always bring what I ordered. But luckily I'm from Minnesota so I figure it's probably what I really wanted anyway.

One December a few years back I was flying home to Minnesota from a whirlwind European romp. After dancing in the all-night discos of Barcelona, a sudden discovery of my recessive Latin genes, I badly needed some rest from my vacation. The plane circles St. Paul and a familiar sight welcomes me; a white blanket of snow covers the earth. I'm home.

Next to me on the plane are two Spanish women who are looking out the window at the frozen landscape and talking in very concerned tones. This is not home for them. I assure them there is nothing to worry about, it's just weather. The plane lands and as we wait to file out, the rear door opens and in steps a large human form, covered from head to foot in a snowmobile suit, scarves, and mittens. He's there to collect the garbage. There is a white frost-circle where he has been breathing through his mouth and the only exposed flesh is the end of his nose, and it is too-white and frostbitten and raw. His presence has taken the European women aback. One woman asks, "Is it cold?"

"Well," says the form, "I'd wear a coat."

I'm home.

I get in a cab. Instead of going directly home I tell the cabbie to take me to the Uptown Bar, to see what the lads are up to. As we drive I mention it's great to see snow. He sarcastically tells me to feast my eyes. His cab driver identification badge says his name is Said—he's Egyptian—so I ask if he ever gets homesick. "Oh," he says, "very much." I ask him what he misses most and he says his language. He says, "Our language is like music." I ask him to speak for me and he's right, it is music and Said is a wonderful performer. I tell him our language is like music, too, not English per se, but the Minnesotan dialect to me is music. I can see in his eyes a clear look of disbelief. So I decide to help him out, teach him to speak like a Minnesotan. It's a technique based on the method devised by Henry Higgins to help Eliza Doolittle learn proper British in *My Fair Lady*. Dr. Higgins has Eliza repeat, "The rain in Spain falls mainly on the plain."

In this case the dialect is Minnesotan and the sentence is derived from a conversation overheard in a convenience store. It goes like this: "I ain't gonna pay no dollar for a corn muffin that's half dough." Say that five times and you're on your way to speaking with the nuanced, rounded Os of a true northlander.

We arrive at the Uptown. I sit at the bar. Next to me is Larry. He turns to me and says, "I've got fourteen personalities"—and he did, easily—"I got fourteen personalities and each one is in love with her." He points to a waitress. She smiles and it's obvious she's in love with all fourteen of him. I decide to fade into the woodwork and leave the two lovebirds alone.

I sit at another table and take out my Christmas list and run down the names. I want to get my brother-in-law something good because every year whatever I get him, he says, "Well, that's different." "Different" is Minnesotan for "what are you thinking?" This year I decide to get him something that actually is "different" so when he says it I won't feel so bad. For instance, I saw this bird feeder in a magazine that is shaped like Prometheus. You put him on a rock and the bird food goes on his liver and every day the birds come and peck it out. Or there is a bumper sticker with a picture of the Pillsbury Doughboy and an inscription in Gothic letters, "He is Risen." I feel guilty I've put this off 'til the last but "guilt is the gift that keeps on giving."

My favorite gift-giving story is from my friend John Van Orman, who is an ethnomusicologist. It involves a group of aboriginal people in Borneo. John told me of an anthropologist who lived among this group in the wilds of Borneo. They gave dances as gifts—dances to each other, to other villages, to their wives or husbands and children—to show their love. This anthropologist lived there for two years and when it came time to leave they performed a dance especially for him. It was incredible, unlike anything he'd ever seen, and he was very moved. He decided to return the favor. It happened he was quite a virtuoso on the violin and he'd brought his instrument along, so he took it out and played the most difficult piece he knew. When he was done the people were ecstatic, they loved it, but they wondered if he "could do it again only this time without making that hideous noise?" I guess that's their version of "well, that's different."

I look around the bar and spot an elderly woman sitting by herself in a Naugahyde booth. She must be in her eighties or nineties and very dressed to the nines: pink and black Jackie O. suit and a matching pillbox hat and drinking tea. Tea. Very out of place in the Uptown Bar. Our eyes meet but instead of looking away, like I usually do (and perhaps due to the recessive Latin gene), I walk up to her. When she looks up at me, her eyebrows disappear under her wig. She feels this and gently and very delicately pulls the wig back. I ask if I can join her and she says, "Of course," like she has been expecting me. As I take a seat across from her she tells me her name is Rose. We pass the next two hours talking about everything under the sun. I tell her about my trip to

Spain, she tells me about her travels and how her husband invented the Frisbee—but back in the 1930s it was called a saucer-tosser—and she has the prototype hanging in her bathroom. I tell her one time on a train I met the guy who invented the fragrance for Halston perfume and Rit Dye number three. "Well," she says, "don't we have interesting lives." I agree, "Yes, Rose, we do." At one point I noticed Rose has a brooch on her lapel, shaped like a lamb. The fleece is rows of pearls. In the middle of the lamb one of the pearls is missing. I ask Rose about her brooch. "Oh," she says, "this is my lucky pin."

She says, "Whenever something terrible happens to me I take out a pearl."

I say, "Rose, there's a pearl missing."

She smiles and says, "Yes, but look how many I have left."

When her tea is finished, she tells me she must be getting home. I help her to the door while Larry bursts into "Blue Christmas."

One of his fourteen personalities is Elvis. Rose says, "He's very good," and he is. I walk Rose to the bus stop and we wait together in silence. When her bus comes I help her aboard. Suddenly she turns and says, "I live in a residence home and I go out maybe twice a year. Once a year during Hanukkah, I make a deal with myself. I won't go home until I have made a new friend." She smiles and says, "And now I can go home." I watch her as her bus pulls away then walk home, where I'll pull out my tuba and practice my gift for my brother-in-law.

racing toward solace

I believe each of us is drawn to a geography whether it's mountains, the desert, or an ocean. There lives in a particular nature that which provides us solace but also awakens our muse.

For me it's the forests and lakes in northern Minnesota.

I was recently up north in the Boundary Waters of Canada and the U.S. on a dog sledding trip. Now, this was my first time dog sledding. We have two wiener dogs, and the thought of a dog doing what I told it to do thrills me to no end.

I'm touring with an outfitter called Wilderness Inquiry. As we drive north past Lake Superior, then inland toward the border, we see a bald eagle, whitetail deer, and a very rare sighting—a timber wolf following the tracks of the deer we just saw.

One in our group, named Sindibad, talks about the spirits of things. For all of us, there is an outside spirit and an inside spirit. The outside is what the world sees and the inside is what we ourselves see. Sindibad sings an Ojibwe song that translates to:

> Here comes the spirit of the wolf
> Here comes the *spirit* of the wolf
> Here comes the spirit of the *wolf*
> Here *is* the spirit of the wolf.

I know from years of coming up here as a kid this land is unforgiving—one mistake can cost a limb or a life. The Boundary Waters Canoe Area is over a million acres of wilderness, its rocky terrain and thousands of miles of lakes formed by receding glaciers. There are no motorized vehicles allowed and visitors are strictly regulated, making it one of the most beautiful, wild places on the planet. This is also winter, where subzero temperatures are common and skin is often referred to as "exposed flesh."

Living in the moment is essential.

About half of our group is from Australia. There are eleven of them from Adelaide, in South Australia. Most of them have never seen snow. They're laughing, completely oblivious to the world that awaits them. I feel like

Hunter S. Thompson in the opening of *Fear and Loathing in Las Vegas*. When he notices his Samoan lawyer hasn't seen the savage winged lizards dive-bombing their car, Thompson says, "Poor bastard will see them soon enough."

Australians are a lot like Americans. I've heard that people who are risk-takers have what's called a "long gene," a genetic predisposition that's housed in the rebellious types who settled our two countries. Unlike Americans I find the Australians have a lack of cynicism that's very refreshing. At first it's hard to get used to—like, "what's their angle?"—but it turns out there is no angle. They are simply more open, there is more sky on their faces. They remind me of how we Americans think we are, like maybe we were when there was more elbow room.

There is a wonderful story. It's a Nazrudin story, the wise fool from Sufi lore. Nazrudin is working in his field and a traveler passes and asks, "What is the next town like?"

Nazrudin asks the traveler, "What is the town like where you are from?"

"Oh," said the man. "One must be very careful. Its full of thieves and cutthroats."

Nazrudin says, "It's the same with this town."

"Thank you," says the traveler. "I'll keep that in mind."

NOT LONG AFTER that another traveler approaches Nazrudin. He too asks, "What is the next town like?"

Nazrudin asks the traveler, "What is the town like where you are from?"

"Oh, its beautiful. The people are the friendliest, most loving souls you'll ever meet."

"It's the same in this town," says Nazrudin.

WHEN WE ARRIVE at the end of the road the Aussies jump right out—somehow they adapt quickly to the frozen north. I guess they're used to living in extremes, only where they're from it's the heat that'll get you. At first the Australians have a tendency to fall down—they keep looking skyward like an answer lives up there—but the cold isn't getting to them.

We are told we must trek across a frozen lake in the dark to the lodge. They aren't too keen about walking across a lake; they maintain walking on water is saved for their deities. I tell them the secret to walking on ice—"have somebody else go first." That's how I got to lead the expedition.

They can't believe how much water we have—their largest lake can expect water every ten years or so. Still they're marked on the map as lakes. I remember a buddy of mine who bought some land in Minnesota only to discover he'd bought a lake . . . full of water. We walk to the lodge, the stars so low I'm hunting with Orion and cartwheeling with Cassiopeia.

The next day I awake and prepare for the outdoors: no cotton—use wool or synthetic fibers, they breathe—and many layers, the last one to block wind. I can't find my boots. For some reason boots are up for grabs with this group. Every day I will have a different pair of boots.

That morning we meet the dogs. Some of them are veterans of the Iditarod, the 1,200-mile race in Alaska. One dog has finished in second place twice. I feel like I'm meeting the canine Michael Jordan. The dogs howl in anticipation.

The Ogalala people say those centuries ago a chasm formed between humans and animals. As it widened at the last minute the Dog left his cousin Wolf and jumped across to be with the humans. The Ogalala feel the mournful cry of the wolf is the longing that the chasm will someday be closed. We hook up the dogs and get ready to go.

WILDERNESS INQUIRY specializes in wilderness trips for people with and without disabilities. In our group and the group from Australia, there are people with a wide variety of disabilities: some of our members are blind, others have Down Syndrome, there are those with brain injury . . . the list is varied, each person unique with his or her own blessings and curses. Nearly everyone in our group sports a challenge but the counselors are unfazed. Everyone has one thing in common: we all want to know "how far can I go?"

I've secretly wanted to drive a sled but wasn't going to complain if I rode in the basket. I have a paralyzed arm and a congenital condition with the left, so hanging on could be an issue. But it's not an issue; I am not only allowed but expected to drive a sled. My enthusiasm is soon overridden by concern.

Often I buy into what the outside world thinks of me . . . mostly based on limitations. They see what I can't do instead of what I can. Like Sindibad said every living creature has a form we see and one we don't. It's true, how we perceive ourselves is rarely as others perceive us and we are all the hero of our own stories. I hope.

When I learned I was to drive at first I was excited but then reality sets in. Will I be able? We are given instructions on how to start, how to go left, how to go right. There is a "brake," a piece of cyclone fencing you step on with your foot, and an emergency brake that's a treble hook on a rope that may or may not catch onto something. Honestly, the brake system is more suggestion than science.

It's been years since I've been this nervous; people, including myself, keep protecting me but now it's time to "see what I'm made of." I step on the runners, lift the brake, and . . . "Let's go!"

The dogs are magnificent. Once running they stop barking and settle into work mode. We are a team, from the powerful wheel dogs in the rear to the lead dogs in front. Their athleticism is now evident, there is obvious joy as they run. This is why they were barking with anticipation. And we are going fast. Not since my days on a motorbike have I experienced such a thrill. That flow of body and nature, where my inside self and my outside self are one. The master and the student at the same time as the samurai say, in one body. . . in control *and* at the mercy of the next moment. More a matter of dancing than hanging on or steering. And it's silent, only the slight *swoosh* as the runners slide over snow.

> Here comes the spirit of the wolf
> Here comes the spirit of the wolf
> Here is the spirit of the wolf.

THAT NIGHT IN THE LODGE we have a talent show. The group I'm with is called Interact, a company specializing in performers with disabilities, and the Australians are from a similar company called Tutti. The talent show rocks. Amy, from Australia, and Sam, from Minnesota, sing a duet a la *West Side Story*. Joel plays the didgeridoo. The didgeridoo, or *yidaki*, is an Australian musical instrument developed in the north of Australia. It's a hollow tube formed as termites eat the tree from the center. It's then cut off at lengths of a couple feet to over six feet, depending upon the desired pitch. To play it you buzz your lips into one end. It's a haunting beautiful drone probably not heard very often in the far north.

Steve, who is indigenous Australian, tells a story of how his people saved the world using *indiginuety*. Even the counselors get in on it. Mark talks of the voyageurs, the French explorers who three hundred years ago traded up here, worked like mad, sang, smoked pipes on the hour, carried ninety-pound packs, and were actually into fashion.

The talent show breaks out into improv sets, using actors from both sides of the world. I'm reminded of King

Lear's fool, or the *heyokas* of the Dakota and Lakota, or the contraries for the Ojibwe, thought of as healers and vision-aries. In cultures around the world the wise fools were used as counsel because they had a foot in two worlds, a height-ened existence. Maybe that's why this group takes to this adventure. A heightened state is a comfortable one.

As I watch the performers work through and beyond their physical limitations I'm struck by the truth and joy, the living in the moment that is at the heart of all great performance.

We tell more stories and then go outside and make snow angels, teaching the Aussies how to drop on your back in a snowbank and wave your arms up and down. You've never seen more unique snow angels than from this group. Then one of the counselors cuts a hole in the lake with a chain saw. Everyone piles into the sauna and then when the heat becomes unbearable, one by one people rush into the freez-ing lake. I am amazed that of the eleven Australians ten jump in, the only abstainer stopping at the last second, claiming, "My mom would not like this."

The evening moves back into the lodge, with fires and more stories as the snow falls outside and softens reality. I feel at home among fellow fools. In these days where the news has become entertainment and entertainment, news, we get the truth where we can find it. A story, or a place of solace.

BACK IN THE DAYS when pots and pans could talk—which indeed they still do—there lived a man. In order to have water every day he had to walk down the hill and fill two pots and walk them home. One day it was discovered one of the pots had a crack and as time went on the crack widened. Finally the pot turned to the man and said, "Every day you take me to the river. By the time you get home half of the water has leaked out. Please replace me with a better pot."

The man said, "You don't understand—as you spill you water the wild flowers by the side of the path." Sure enough on the side of the path where the cracked pot was carried beautiful flowers grew, while the other side was barren.

"I think I'll keep you," said the man.

WE LEAVE THE NEXT MORNING. Lo and behold, the remaining boots are my own.

Riding in the van I hear the Australians telling their stories. It seems in every new rendition the cold is mentioned and the temperature drops another ten degrees. As we drive through the forest there is a new energy in the van. We're not the same people we were three days ago.

We ride past Lake Superior in silence.

Here comes the spirit of the wolf. . . .

rio

I knew when my dad invited me over for a pancake breakfast it meant two things. One, I have to eat at least ten pancakes or it's not even worth it to make the batter. And two, when I'm done a semi-truck full of industrial paint will pull into the driveway and need to be unloaded.

I've eaten my ten pancakes. We wait for the semi. In my pocket I have a tape from a new performance art group I'm in. It is headbanging music, loud and offensive and angry, and I know it will piss off my dad. I play the tape for Dad and he smiles and says, "Things seem to be going well for you, Kev." The semi never comes and my dad tells me he has cancer. He says, "Kevin, it's not immediately life-threatening. I'm gonna be around for a long time."

I get on a plane and fly to Rio de Janeiro. Rio-de-Janeiro. Rio-by-the-sea-o.

Ipanema, Copacabana. Beautiful beaches, beautiful people walking by. And I'm thinking, "My cat plays with more cloth than is on this beach."

I'm watching my girlfriend swim at the hotel beach. Next to me is this huge German guy. He looks like the Michelin Man. Next to him is this thin, pale, paid traveling companion. He's got this look on his face like, "I'm not getting paid enough." The Michelin Man is looking at my girlfriend and says, "Why do you bring your girlfriend to Rio de Janeiro? Zat's like bringing a sandwich to a bar-b-que."

The city of Rio is stretching up behind me, up to the statue of Christ: Corcavada. A man I've met at the hotel comes up and says, "We have a beautiful city, do we not?"

I say, "Oh yes, it's incredible!"

He says, "You see those buildings up there, the blue and the white and the yellow?" I say, "Yeah. Very nice."

He says, "Don't go up to those buildings. Those buildings are the slums. Stay away from them, they are very dangerous. But we paint them nice for you tourists. What do you think? Aren't they beautiful?"

I decide to look at the beach instead. I say, "Why don't the locals swim down here? Why don't you swim in Ipanema or Copacabana?"

He said, "Well, sometimes after the rain, the sewage from the slums washes down into the water and sometimes if the tide isn't right, it will wash up onto the beach. Not always."

Watching my girlfriend swim in the surf, the Michelin Man says, "Have you been to the Scala?"

I say, "What?"

"Have you been to the Scala? It is a nightclub act. Each act more spectacular than the last. I cry like a child."

I think, "I gotta see what makes this guy cry like a child." So that night we go to the Scala, this nightclub in the middle of the jungle. It looks like a piece of Las Vegas with neon signs out front. Inside is a huge stage with giant speakers. A tiny man comes out with a sequined high hat and white sequined suit. "*Mein damen und herren;* Ladies and Gentlemen. Welcome to the Scala! Waah!" His eyes and mouth are wide open. These women come dancing out with feathered hats that are twice as tall as they are. They are balancing them on their heads and have bare breasts. Every time their bare breasts pass this man's little head, he shouts, "Waah! Waah! Scala! Scala!" Then he introduces a Rio do Janeiro quica band. They come out with their quicas and their drums and their maracas. They're piped through those huge speakers and they're turned up so loud, they start beating my heart for me. I yell to my girlfriend, "We've got to get out of here."

The next day we rent a car. By evening we leave the city proper. People are driving by, but their headlights aren't on. Their headlights are off. I ask someone later, "Why do people drive without their headlights?"

They said, "They think it wastes gas."

The cars are going past, flashing their lights like "Your

lights are on! Your lights are on!" "I know my lights are on. I'm trying to see."

We're driving down the road. It starts to rain, a light, tropical rain. "Whoa!" The car starts to slide. The mud is sliding down the hill. Pretty soon it's hard to hold the car on the road. My girlfriend says, "Why don't we pull over for the night?" I'm fighting to keep the car on the road. Now the mud isn't just going under the car, it's going up over the car. I turn on the windshield wipers, but they just smear it on the window. I roll down my window so I can see. Just then the hillside comes sliding down behind us and wipes out the road. "Okay, wherever we're going, that's where we're staying!"

At daybreak, we get to this little village. These people come out of their houses. They see us and they go back inside. They come out again. This time they have card tables. They set them up, look at us, and go back inside. This time they come out with stuffed, mounted animals. They set them on the card tables up and down this street, and say, "Come buy. Come buy. Buy this. Buy this!" I'm looking at these animals and they all have blue eyes. Big blue glass eyes. I wondered what happened. Did a crate wash up on shore filled with blue glass eyes and they started stuffing everything they could get their hands on? There were turtles with big blue eyes, parrots, little dogs—all with big blue eyes. I looked at those blue glass eyes and the brown-eyed people selling them. "Buy this!" My girlfriend has her window down and is giggling and petting the animals. I say,

"We gotta get out of here. We gotta get out of this place. This isn't paradise. This is a nightmare!"

We're driving toward Rio in the night. The car slips in the mud and threatens to slip down into the jungle. A light drizzle begins to fall.

I'm three years old, leaning against my dad, smelling him in his cotton shirt. I'm in the front seat of our car eating an ice cream cone and holding my blanket. "Where are we going, Dad?"

I'm lying in a puddle of water working with my dad on his airplane. He says, "You know, Kev, the day you were born I was in the garage putting the wings on a Piper Cub. I rushed to the hospital and held you for the first time with airplane goop and dope dripping off my hands."

I'm with my dad. We're waiting for the semi. I've just eaten my tenth pancake. I play him the tape and he smiles.

When grandmother drove into the driveway, she saw all of grandfather's tools put away. She went into the house and dialed 911 for the paramedics. Grandmother had never seen those tools put away. She knew my grandpa's time had come.

My grandpa was hit with lightning when he was with his tools. My brother, who has four motorcycles, three snowmobiles, a couple of cars, and a few boats, was hit while he was pumping gas. My dad was hit when he was with his airplane. He loved to fly. More than anything else in his life, he loved to fly. My dad was hit with his airplane . . . but he was also hit with me.

I get home from Rio and my father is still in the hospital. I'm with him one night and he gets out of bed. He doesn't show it but I know he's been in a lot of pain. I'm afraid he's going to pull the IV out of his arm so I get up and he says, "Sit down." Then he takes out a suitcase, a suitcase only he could see, and he packs his belongings, sets it down, and crawls back into bed. That night all the family gathered around a table. A nurse came in and told us Dad was on life-support and the family needed to let him go. "It's the right thing, Kevin. He's in a lot of pain. Even if he does come back he won't be the same."

"No . . ." And while I was saying no, my father passed away.

I remember sitting with him that night and wondering where I'm going to be the next time I get hit by lightning.

the dog says how

Several years ago I was in a motorcycle accident that
made typing difficult, so I invested in voice-activated software for my computer. The voiceware has to get to know
my vocal patterns and inflections so there is a series of sentences I read into the computer and it learns my vocal nu-
ances. I remember when the movie *Fargo* came out people
kept calling my local radio station saying, "Hey, what's the
deal? We don't sound like that."

So I'm reading away when my dog and cat get in a fight.
Bark, bark. Meow, meow, meow. Bark, bark. I look at the com-
puter and it has written: "How how why why why how how."
I think that explains a lot.

I think when it comes to the underworld most people

are either dogs or cats. It's either "How?" or "Why?" For me the underworld is like a good haircut in that it probably falls somewhere between something I have and something I wanted. But you don't know. You do know whenever you take a trip there's the trip you plan and the trip you take. You get out your maps, pack just right . . . but at some point you just have to give in to the ride, give in to the journey. Face it, the only place that looks like its map . . . is Nebraska.

Time was only a select few visited the underworld, like Odysseus, Orpheus, Dante, Nixon. Now anyone with enough money can go to hell. When I had my accident I got a glimpse of things to come. As I lay unconscious I had that experience so often talked about. I never saw "the light," but as doctors were working to save my life, I was heading for this amazing sense of peace. At some point I was given the choice to continue on or return to this plane of existence where it was made clear there *would* be consequences. I did return but without the use of my right arm. At first it bothered me that I had returned. Why didn't I follow that peace?

But it's too late to turn back; I'd returned to the living. At least I thought I had. There was a guy who saw the accident who thought I had died. He went around telling people I had died and even to this day he still believes it. I've seen him on the bus a few times and have tried to talk to him, but he looks right through me. He honestly thinks I am a ghost.

At first this was disconcerting. But he's right. I haven't completely returned—I can't. But I've grown used to the fact that I do have a foot in two worlds. So now I haunt and am haunted.

And let's face it. We all have things that haunt us: ghosts, things that can't find a home, that go bump in our hearts and minds. We call them names like Sins or Regrets or Desires. They seem to fall into two categories: kind of like Kentucky Fried Chicken—they're either original or extra spicy. Original ones are with us from before birth, tiny time bombs lurking in our genetic weedbed, just waiting to spring into acts of passion or illness. We can't do anything about them. We don't even know why they're there—like the tae kwon do school in a shopping mall. (Why is that there? It just is.) Then there are the haunts we create by losses or choices made in life. They tend to trouble us even more. Our great fear is that they will follow us into the afterlife.

Dante understood this. When he entered the underworld midway through life, he called it *Dis*. D-i-s, Latin for the underworld, the place of shadow and reflection, a place to contemplate and round off the rough edges of torment and desire. He knew you can't cure a trauma, whether it's a broken limb or heart or promise. The heart, especially, is an instrument that once broken never plays the same and, although it can't be cured, it can be healed.

Dante knew *Dis* was a necessary step toward paradise. It's also the prefix for words like *dis*ability, which doesn't mean *un*ability. It means able in a different way. Able through the world of shadow and reflection. A foot in two worlds. *Dis*.

We have a Basset Hound we got as a puppy. We were told by the breeder that when training a Basset Hound they start out slow and then taper off. If ours sees a squirrel he goes crazy and runs after it. But if the squirrel goes up a tree, the dog thinks, "Wow, it's gone. How? How, how? How? How?" And there's the squirrel in the tree looking down at his problem.

Ever since my accident I don't fear death. I get a sense of peace to think I'll see my ancestors and friends I've lost—and my dad, my dog, and my arm. Until then . . . How how why why why.

acknowledgments

My family, Von, Dora, Laura, Steven, I love you.

I would like to express my gratitude to the folks at Borealis Books: Pam McClanahan and Greg Britton. And to Bill Holm, John Rezmerski, Mary Ludington, Mary McGeheran, Steven Dietz, Mark Bly, Kenneth Washington, David Esbjornson, Erin Sanders, and Michael Dixon. And all those at Jungle Theater, The Guthrie, Second Stage, Seattle Rep, and the National Storytelling Festival in Jonesborough, Tennessee. Also National Public Radio's *All Things Considered*, Noah Adams and Bob Boilen, Minnesota Public Radio, Tony Bohl and Leif Larsen, Susan Schulman, Amy Bissonette, John Richardson, Patty Lynch, Jim Stowell, Michael Sommers, Loren "Dr. Buzz" Niemi, Rob Simonds, Lynda Barry, Will Ackerman, Julie Boyd, and the doctors and nurses at HCMC.

And finally, Jon Spelman and the teachers at Osseo High School and Gustavus Adolphus College for pointing the way.

The Dog Says How was designed and set in type by Percolator Graphic Design, Minneapolis. The type is Adobe Chaparral, designed by Carol Twombly. Printed by Maple Press, York, Pennsylvania.